Cooperative Research and Reports

by Murray Suid

Illustrated by Marilynn G. Barr

This book is for
Frank McCulloch

Publisher: Roberta Suid
Editor: Annalisa Suid
Design: Jeffrey Goldman
Production: Santa Monica Press
Educational consultant: Sue Krumbein

Other books by the author: *Cooperative Language Arts,*
Book Factory, Editing, Greeting Cards, Letter Writing,
More Book Factory, Picture Book Factory, Research, Sentences, Stories,
Writing Hangups, How to Be President of the U.S.A.

ISBN 1-878279-50-5

Printed in the United States of America

9 8 7 6 5 4 3 2

Contents

Introduction

- The Apollo mission to the moon
- The evening news
- The discovery of DNA
- The publication of the book you hold in your hands

Real-world projects like these almost always involve teamwork. Even when one person gets all the credit, the achievement usually was a group effort. A good example is Thomas Edison. While he's popularly thought of as the sole inventor of the light bulb, that achievement was a group effort. In fact, some historians believe that Edison's greatest invention was the idea of team research.

Cooperation doesn't mean ignoring solo creativity and individual responsibility. One of the main goals of shared learning is to bring out the best in each person.
There's another bonus: when your students become adept at encouraging and teaching each other, your job will become a lot easier, and more rewarding.

REAL-WORLD FORMS OF COOPERATION

The activities in this book are based on real-world models. For example, "Classroom Curators" was inspired by the kind of work done by museum managers. All of the projects fit into one or more of the following categories:

- **Team cooperation:** The given task naturally requires participants to play a variety of roles. For example, when putting on a trial, there will be a judge, a recorder, a prosecutor, a defense attorney, and jurors. All of these people must work together in order to see that justice is done.

- **Shared-role cooperation:** Two or more people carry out a single task. A well-known example is the team of Woodward and Bernstein, the reporters who broke the Watergate story. But the same side-by-side approach works equally well in science research in which two or more investigators try to replicate a given experiment.

Next, we'll visit the Geo-center.

- **Creator-audience cooperation:** Most reporters consider their work finished only when the report is read or seen by someone. That's why it's so important in the classroom to have most whole-language activities culminate in "publishing," whether done live (orally), on tape, or on paper.

Cooperative learning can be wonderfully varied. The popular image is of several students sitting at a table, helping each other master a skill or body of knowledge. This is a valid approach, and there are many examples of it in the pages of this book. But it is only one of many options.

These options become apparent with the following definition: *cooperative learning is an activity in which two or more students contribute to the end result.* The students can be working together, side by side, or their efforts may be sequential, as when one child writes a script and two others perform it. It's even possible for students in this year's class to cooperate with students from the past or even the future. (See "Electronic Time Capsule" and "Pass-it-on Learning.")

THE SKILLS OF COOPERATION

Cooperative learning doesn't happen by accident. It is an art. This book is about helping children master the exciting skills of collaboration, many of which echo the processes found in the whole-language approach. These include:

- setting goals
- breaking a job into manageable chunks
- listening and speaking
- sharing resources
- giving and taking feedback
- teaching
- compromising
- evaluating
- producing things that have intrinsic value

I'm your Time Capsule host.

Students will have many chances to practice these skills in the context of authentic research and reporting.

TEACHING THE ACTIVITIES

Most of the projects can easily be adapted to all subject areas. Many, such as "Object Interviews," require only a modest amount of time and readily available materials. A few, for example, "Model Thinking" and "Television Documentary," provide greater challenges and involve the use of camcorders and other modern learning tools.

You'll find easy-to-follow, step-by-step directions for presenting every activity. In many cases, reproducible worksheets further clarify the given task. In addition, for some of the interactive projects, such as the "Biographical Interview," model scripts enable novices to sample the activity before trying it themselves. Many of the activities involve acting, drawing, and using other communication techniques. The Resources section offers a variety of tips to help students achieve quality results in these areas.

WHERE TO BEGIN

If your students have already had successful cooperative learning experiences, then you might begin with any project that interests you and fits your curricular needs. On the other hand, if your students need to learn the basics of cooperative learning, then try the following "teamwork warmups."

- Read about cooperation. To help students realize that cooperation extends beyond the school, read aloud stories featuring real-world collaborators, such as the Curies and the Wright brothers.

- Invite guests to visit your classroom and talk about how they learn and work together. These people might include team researchers from a local college, planning committees from city hall, and reporters and producers from a TV station.

- Create a bulletin board or handout that highlights the do's and don'ts of cooperation. (See page 9 for ideas.)

Do's and Don'ts of Cooperation

TEACHER TIPS FOR COOPERATIVE SUCCESS

1. Keep groups small.

Self-managing large groups requires maturity and practice. Therefore, especially at first, provide many two-person group experiences. Pairs usually have an easier time helping each other. Also, in a pair each partner is likely to make a contribution. (There's no place to hide.)

2. Make sure everyone understands the task.

Post a set of directions or list them on a handout. As students become experienced, have them create their own "to do lists" for you to check. When an assignment involves a new format, consider doing it first as a whole-group activity. Model the work at the front of the room. With written work, provide models. For example, if students are writing a television documentary script, give them samples. Explain that you don't want them to copy the content, but only to use the structure (how the character names are laid out, where the dialogue goes, and so on).

3. Monitor progress along the way.

As your own experience on teams should demonstrate, cooperative work can bog down at times. Indeed, learning how to deal with interactive difficulties is a major reason for giving students cooperative experiences. By sitting in on groups, you will be able to help students identify problems before they become calamities. Points to look for include:

- Involvement: Is everyone getting a chance to share?
- Responsibility: Is everyone shouldering the load?
- Helpfulness: Are stronger members willing to help those who are struggling?

Sometimes, what you observe can be shared with the whole class in terms of generic comments. You might even talk about your own experiences in groups.

The history of soap goes back at least 2000 years. Tribes in Germany blended wood ashes and...

Our report is about soap and water.

4. Emphasize quality over quantity.

Few young students can produce long and high-quality stories, speeches, or other work. If you don't provide limits, students will often churn out boring, error-filled work. By giving restrictions—a two-page observation report, a five-minute panel presentation—you're likely to see better work. Note that in the worlds of publishing and TV, almost all work is done to strict time or length limits.

5. Foster self-evaluation by clearly stating the "criteria for success."

Don't have students guess what you look for in a bulletin board, mime show, letter, or whatever. By explicitly listing what you expect, you give students a better chance to perform up to expectations. Handing out an evaluation sheet can also help. As students become more adept at self-evaluation, they may be able to create their own evaluation forms. In addition to evaluating their products, you'll probably want students to assess the process they went through. To help them take stock of their cooperative efforts, give them a "Group Process Checklist" like the one on page 10.

Do's and Don'ts of Cooperation

Make sure everyone agrees on what your team is trying to do.

Be ready to learn from your partner or group.

Be willing to share your knowledge and your ideas.

Listen carefully to what others say. Don't interrupt.

Offer help when someone in the group is having trouble with a task.

Ask for help if you're having trouble.

Don't blame others when things go wrong. Put your energy into solving problems.

Try different roles in a group. Don't always go for the most glamorous job.

When giving feedback (telling others how they're doing), be as specific as possible. Instead of saying, "Good acting job," try "Your voice was loud and clear."

Work hard. Do your share . . . and more.

Group Process Checklist

My name:_____

Others in my group:_____

_____

Type of project: _____

Date project was completed:_____

Steps we went through in completing our project:_____

_____

_____

Strong points about our group (for example, "We listened well to each other"): _____

_____

_____

Weak points about our group (ways we could have worked better as a team):_____

_____

_____

Advice I'd give to anyone else who might try this project:_____

_____

_____

_____

Activities

BIOGRAPHICAL INTERVIEWS

By combining imagination with research, students can create up-close and personal reports of famous people. The task gives practice in asking questions and writing scripts. You might want to present a model interview for students. Invite the principal, custodian, or librarian into the classroom as your interview subject.

DIRECTIONS:

1. Each student gathers information about a well-known historical or contemporary figure. Students might all choose from a single category such as "famous scientists" or "early citizens of our town." Or have them pick figures from a variety of fields. They can use the "Biographical Fact Form" (page 13) to organize their facts.

2. Students write TV-style scripts in which their subjects are interviewed. Using the information gathered, students imagine how their subjects might answer questions. The script should include a brief introduction. (See model on page 14.)

3. Divide the class into pairs to rehearse the scripts. Each script-writer will play the famous person. The partner will act the role of the interviewer.

4. After sufficient rehearsal, partners take turns "interviewing" each other in front of the class or on videotape. In some cases, it might be appropriate for the interviewee to wear a simple costume based on a picture of the person obtained during the research.

EXTENSION:

Students interview each other about their own areas of expertise. For example, one student might possess a great deal of knowledge about playing the trombone. Another might have firsthand information about fishing, dancing, or collecting baseball cards.

Ms. Potter, how did you think up the "Tale of Peter Rabbit."

You may call me Beatrix.

Biographical Fact Form

Name of researcher: _____

Name of person who will be researched: _____

What the person is most famous for: _____

_____

Person's birth date: _____

Person's birthplace: _____

Person's current age or age at death: _____

Tell how the person got interested in the activity that made him or her
famous (use more paper if needed):

_____

_____

Describe one or more difficult problems that the person had to solve:

_____

_____

_____

List at least three questions that people might like to ask the person:

_____

_____

_____

Interview Script

THE INVENTOR OF TELEVISION

Interviewer: (faces audience) Today I'll be talking to Philo Farnsworth, who helped invent TV. (faces Philo) Mr. Farnsworth . . .

Philo: Please call me "Philo."

Interviewer: OK, Philo, why did you become an inventor?

Philo: While growing up in Utah, I read about inventors and wanted to be like them.

Interviewer: How did you dream up television?

Philo: When I was 11, we moved to an Idaho farm. I found some old magazines which told how people were trying to use electricity to send pictures from place to place. Two years later I figured out how to do it.

Interviewer: Did you build your first TV right then?

Philo: No, but I shared my ideas with my science teacher. He warned me to keep the plans secret until I could build a working model.

Interviewer: How old were you when you built that model?

Philo: Twenty. Three friends and I spent months in San Francisco working out the details. We sent our first picture on September 7, 1927.

Interviewer: Are you glad you invented television?

Philo: Yes, especially when it's used in science, for example, sending pictures from space.

Interviewer: Our time is up. Thanks for being here.

Philo: You're welcome.

BOOK FORUMS

An important step in becoming a mature researcher is learning that one can find many books on a single subject. The following activity dramatizes that truth in the form of a multi-book "books" report.

DIRECTIONS:

1. Divide the class into small groups. Have each group elect a moderator.
2. Each group should choose a topic on which several nonfiction books have been written. Examples: the space shuttle, dinosaurs, soccer, or rain forests.
3. Each student picks a book on the topic, reads it, and prepares about half a dozen note cards. There should be one important fact or quotation on each card.
4. Group members should share their information, making sure that each member has at least three unique facts to present.
5. At the start of the whole-class presentation, each group's moderator should briefly describe the chosen subject, and then call on forum members to take turns sharing their facts. At times, it may make sense to hold up books to share pictures.
6. When students are done presenting their facts, the moderator might ask for questions from the audience, and then allow panel members to volunteer answers.

EXTENSION:

Forum members can pool their knowledge to make a bulletin board featuring facts from each of their books.

CHAIN LETTER REPORTS

In the culture at large, one researcher's discovery often pushes another investigator to probe deeper. The following activity replicates this process in the classroom.

DIRECTIONS:

1. Have the class brainstorm a list of interesting topics. Make the list long enough so that there's a different topic for everyone in the room.

2. Each student (or small team) picks a topic and does research, then shares a single fact at the beginning of a "To Whom It May Concern" letter. For example, a letter dealing with polar bears might begin with the fact that polar bears cover their black noses with their paws when stalking prey. The source of the fact should be given.

3. Students exchange letters with classmates who are then challenged to add a short paragraph clarifying or expanding on the previous material. For example, the polar bear's diet might be described.

4. After a predetermined period of research (say, two days), each person adds a new fact to the letter, and then does another exchange.

5. After a certain number of exchanges, the letters might be read aloud, published in the school newspaper, displayed on a bulletin board, or bound into a chain letter "trivia" book which can then be circulated among students and parents.

EXTENSION:

Do the same activity as a round-robin activity involving different schools.

CLASS LETTERS

Professional writers and researchers often gather information by going directly to experts. Letter writing is an efficient and exciting way of doing this.

DIRECTIONS:
1. Have the class choose a topic of broad interest, for example, robots, dinosaurs, or boa constrictors.
2. Brainstorm a list of experts or agencies that might have information about the topic. For example, experts on boa constrictors might include: people at a zoo, veterinarians, authors of books on snakes, science reporters who work for the local newspaper, and science teachers at a nearby high school or college. (See page 18 for some helpful addresses.)
3. Have the class work together to compose a letter asking questions about the topic.
4. Mail different versions of the letter to different experts.
5. When a reply comes, write a class thank-you note.

EXTENSION:
Try sending question letters to the letters columns of newspapers. Many classes have been using this technique as a way of discovering facts about other areas of the country, or even about other countries.

17

Where to Write

ABC TV
1330 Ave. of the Americas
New York, NY 10019

Boy Scouts of America
International Letter Exchange
P.O. Box 61030
Dallas/Ft. Worth Airport, TX 75261

Canada Office of Tourism
150 Kent St.
Ottawa, ON
K1A OH6

Canadian Broadcast Corp.
1500 Bronson Ave.
Ottawa, ON
K1G 3J5

CBS TV
51 W. 52nd St.
New York, NY 10019

Environmental Protection Agency
401 M St., SW
Washington, D.C. 20460

Federal Bureau of Investigation
Pennsylvania Ave., NW
Washington, D.C.

House of Representatives
Capitol Building
Washington, D.C. 20515

Major League Baseball
75 Rockefeller Plaza
New York, NY 10020

National Aeronautics & Space
  Administration (NASA)
Johnson Space Center
Houston, TX 77058

National Audubon Society
950 Third Ave.
New York, NY 10022

National Basketball Association
Olympic Tower
645 Fifth Ave.
New York, NY 10022

National Football League
410 Park Ave.
New York, NY 10022

National Science Foundation
1800 G St., NW
Washington, D.C. 20550

National Wildlife Federation
8925 Leesburg Pike
Vienna, VA 22184

NBC TV
30 Rockefeller Plaza
New York, NY 10020

Organization of American States
Constitution Ave. & 17th St., NW
Washington, D.C. 20230

Senate Office Building
Washington, D.C. 20510

CLASS-MADE ENCYCLOPEDIA

No one knows everything. That's why encyclopedia making requires collaboration. By contributing to a classroom encyclopedia, students share their expertise while learning about this important resource.

DIRECTIONS:

1. Have students go on an encyclopedia scavenger hunt. Working alone or in small groups, they can use the "Encyclopedia Hunt" worksheet (page 20).
2. Read aloud several short encyclopedia articles. Point out typical features. (See model on page 21.)
3. Students choose familiar topics, or ones they can investigate firsthand through observation or interviewing. Example: a student living in an apartment building might know different facts about that type of structure. (See page 22 for other topics.)
4. Students draft their articles using the "Encyclopedia Article Planner" (page 23).
5. After polishing the rough drafts, students produce final versions on hole-punched paper that can be bound in a ring binder. This makes it easier to insert fresh articles later on.
6. As a culminating activity, share the information on a class bulletin board, in a group-edited book, or in a TV program.

EXTENSION:

Add to the encyclopedia during the year and in future years. When the binder is full, divide the contents into volumes.

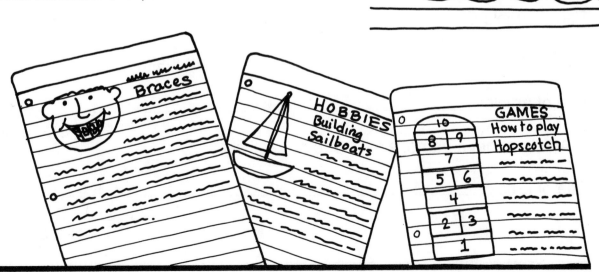

Encyclopedia Hunt

Your name: _____

Title of encyclopedia: _____

Find an example of each kind of encyclopedia article listed below.

1. Article about a person, such as a leader, an inventor, an artist, or an athlete.

Title of article: _____

2. Article about a place where people live. Examples: a city, a state, a province, or a country.

Title of article: _____

3. Article about an ocean, a desert, a mountain, a forest, or a planet.

Title of article: _____

4. Article about an invention.

Title of article: _____

5. Article about one kind of plant or animal.

Title of article: _____

6. Article about events in nature, for example, earthquakes.

Title of article: _____

7. Article about a game, a skill, or other activity.

Title of article: _____

Sample Encyclopedia Article

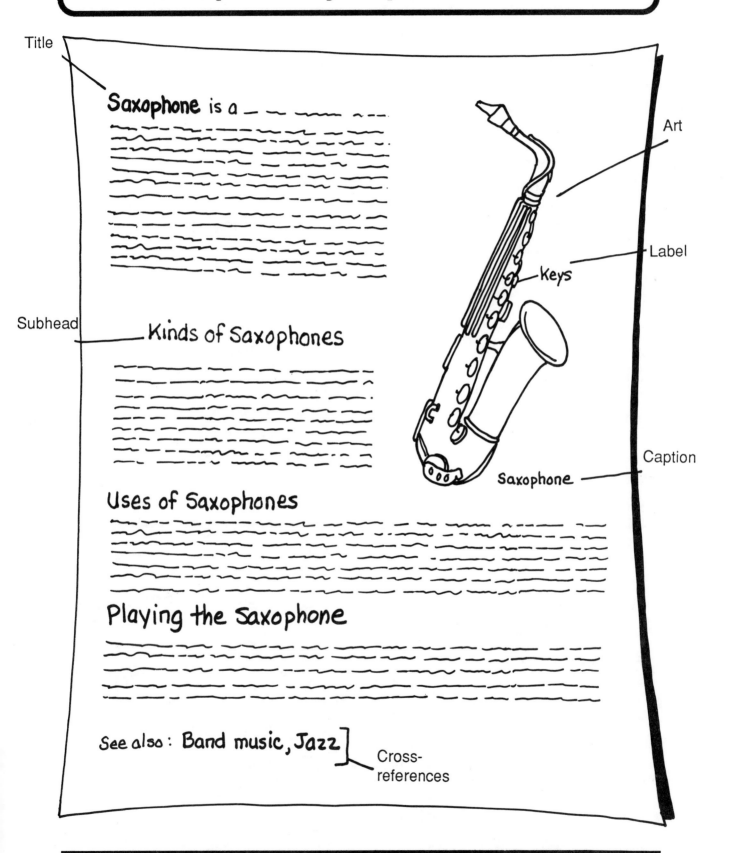

Title

Saxophone is a _ _ _ _ _ _ _ _ _ _ _ _

Art

Label

Keys

Subhead

Kinds of Saxophones

Caption

Saxophone

Uses of Saxophones

Playing the Saxophone

See also: Band music, Jazz

Cross-references

Encyclopedia Article Topics

animals (pets)

apartment building

biographies of:
- classmates
- family members
- friends
- neighbors
- school staff

clubs

computers

family roles

games

gardens

hobbies

holidays

houses

illnesses

model making

musical instruments

parks and playgrounds

places visited on family trips

school building

sports:
- soccer
- horseback riding
- rollerblading

Encyclopedia Article Planner

1. Pick a topic that you know a lot about. Examples: a hobby, a place, or a person such as a music teacher.

2. List several questions that someone might ask about your topic. Use the back of this sheet for more room:

_____

_____

_____

_____

3. If you need information to answer the questions, gather facts by interviewing or observing. Example: If you're doing a report about cats, you might want to tell how cats eat. Watch a cat at its dinner time. Take notes and draw pictures.

4. Start your encyclopedia article with a definition. For example, an article about skateboards might begin:

> **SKATEBOARD** is a slightly-curved board, usually less than three feet (one meter) long, with four wheels. It is used mainly in the sport of skateboarding, but can also be used for transportation.

An article about a person always begins with the person's last name. For example, an article about Mike Hill would begin:

> **HILL, MIKE** is a dentist who works in Palo Alto.

5. Continue with other paragraphs that add details.

6. After polishing your words, copy them in encyclopedia format.

7. Add art (pictures, maps, or diagrams) to help explain your subject.

CLASSROOM CURATORS

There's more to a classroom than meets the casual eye. In the following activity, students tap firsthand experiences to unfold the wonders of their room to guests and future students.

DIRECTIONS:
1. Break the class into four or five small groups.
2. Have each group prepare a short report about an important area of your room or an important ongoing activity. Examples: the media center, a math corner, or a time set aside daily for personal reading. Group members should coauthor a script using the information from the report, and rehearse it in front of the whole class.
3. When visitors come, arrange for your expert guides to shepherd them to the key landmarks, or explain important ongoing activities.

EXTENSION:
Prepare a "This Is Our Classroom" videotape for parents or community guests. At the end of the year, graduating fifth or sixth graders could create a videotape on the various facilities in the school for the next year's incoming students.

DO YOU SEE WHAT I SEE?

Scientists and artists must see accurately. To nurture this skill, have students join observation teams through which they'll compare and contrast their perceptions. This activity also demonstrates that sharing knowledge can produce a clearer picture of reality.

DIRECTIONS:

1. Do a whole-class observation of an object, for example, the flag or your desk. As students point out details, take notes on the board. This will help students understand what to write when they work in small groups.

2. Divide the class into groups of four or five.

3. Arrange for each group to spend a few minutes observing a subject. Examples: a fish in an aquarium, a spider web, a shadow, a cloud-filled sky, or a melting piece of ice. During the session, each student should take notes. (See page 26 for other subjects to observe.)

4. Later, have all group members compare and pool their observations to make a group report. They can use Venn diagrams to distinguish between what they all saw and what was seen only by some students.

EXTENSION:

Have students do group perception activities using other senses, for example, hearing or touching.

Subjects to Observe

animals:
- fish in an aquarium
- fly on a wall
- bird in a tree
- butterfly on a flower

athletes on a playground

children on a playground

face (live, photograph)

microscopic image:
- hair
- piece of paper

painting

physical phenomenon:
- ball rolling down an inclined plane
- bicycle wheel spinning
- dye mixing into clear water

scene outside classroom window

someone performing an action:
- combing hair
- reading
- juggling
- making a sandwich
- sharpening a pencil

videotape excerpt from any educational program

weather:
- sunny sky
- clouds
- fog
- rain
- snow

ELECTRONIC TIME CAPSULE

People have been making time capsules for a long time. Here's an up-to-date way for students to share their knowledge with those who come after them.

DIRECTIONS:

1. Explain the project to the students. Talk about how some time capsules, containing clothing, books, and other objects, are buried deep in the ground in water-proof containers designed to keep the items safe for decades.

2. Divide the class into several groups. Each group should choose a curriculum-related topic that you've been studying. Examples: dinosaurs, word problems, China, or current events.

3. The groups gather information on their topics. Material can come from textbooks, reports students have given, interviews with experts, or other sources.

4. Depending on equipment available, teams prepare scripts for an audio or video report. The scripts should contain speaking parts for everyone. (See the "TV Time Capsule Planner," page 28, and a model script, page 29.) Have groups practice their reports until they feel comfortable with their presentations.

5. Record the reports onto a single audio or video tape. If you're doing a TV time capsule, encourage students to look directly into the camera as they speak.

6. Have students review their presentations and make any corrections if necessary.

7. Date the cassette and its container. Add a note that the "capsule" should be played by next year's class.

8. A year later, share the tape with your new students so that they can compare and contrast their learning experiences with those of learners from the past.

EXTENSION:

Produce imaginary time capsule programs from the past, for example, from the year Edison introduced his light bulb.

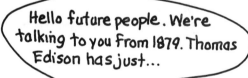

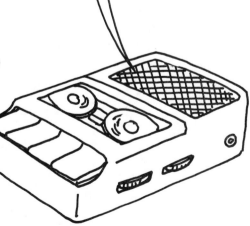

TV Time Capsule Planner

( ) **Step 1.** Pick a topic that's been studied in the classroom, for example, recycling.

( ) **Step 2.** Choose the host and crew for the program. The crew will include camera person, sound person, lighting person, and others who will work hard to make the show run smoothly.

( ) **Step 3.** Break the big topic into several smaller topics (called "subtopics"). For example, recycling might cover paper, glass, cans, and garbage.

( ) **Step 4.** Decide who will handle each subtopic.

( ) **Step 5.** For each subtopic, think up something to show the camera. Remember: TV viewers like to look at interesting things.

( ) **Step 6.** Write the script—the words that you'll say.

( ) **Step 7.** Rehearse the words while pointing to whatever you plan to show the viewers.

( ) **Step 8.** Make the tape.

Time Capsule TV Script

(This one-page sample is from a longer script.)

Ellen

Hello. My name is Ellen. I am your Time Capsule host. My classmates and I are sending you this tape from Mrs. Gritzer's class in the year 1987 to give you some examples of what we are studying. Now, the Science Team will tell you about several science activities going on in the room.

Victor

This month, NASA launched a satellite to explore the rings of Saturn. (Points to pictures of Saturn) As you can see from our Space Bulletin Board, we have been making our own sketches of that planet.

Tracy

(Points to a telescope) The PTA purchased this telescope for the school. We have been learning how to use it. Later this month, we will have an evening session when students and parents will have a chance to use it to look at the moon.

Norma

(Points to the aquarium) We are also learning about things closer to earth. Our classroom aquarium lets us study how snails keep the water clean.

Don

(Holds up a computer disk) We've been writing letters to real scientists to learn more about brand-new discoveries.

Ellen

(Faces Don) Thank you, Don, and the rest of the science team. (Faces the camera) You can see that we have been busy with science. But we have been doing lots of other activities as well. Now it's time to meet our current events team.

I'm your Time Capsule host.

FACT CHECKING

At magazines such as *Time* and *Newsweek*, someone checks the facts in every article. For example, a writer may say that "Mice and giraffes have an equal number of neck bones." To make sure that the statement is true, the fact checker will open a book or call the zoo. In school, this kind of double-checking provides excellent research practice. It also allows students to help each other.

DIRECTIONS:

1. Each student prepares a short report containing at least three facts that most people wouldn't know. For example, a paper about weather might include the fact that a 1928 hurricane killed 1,836 people in Florida.

2. Students should number and underline their key facts and give the source for each one. The sources can be listed at the bottom of the page or on a separate piece of paper. (See model on page 31.)

3. Students exchange papers with a partner.

4. Partners "fact check" each other's report using the "Fact-Checking Worksheet" (page 32). They can go to the same sources the author used or different sources.

5. The completed worksheet should be attached to the report and returned to the author. If the fact checker discovered any possible fact errors, the author should consult another source and make needed corrections.

EXTENSION:

For a more challenging exercise, the authors should not list their sources. This way, the fact checkers will have to locate sources on their own.

Is this the mayor's office? I need to know how much money...

Sample Report with Surprising Facts

THE TRUTH ABOUT KING KONG

King Kong is one of the most famous film characters of all time. Kong was first seen in a black-and-white movie that came out in 1933. (1) In that movie, Kong was really an 18-inch model. (2) Many years later, the film was remade in color. This time, in most of the scenes, Kong was played by an actor wearing a gorilla suit.

Both of these movies were very scary. They made many people think that gorillas are the most dangerous animals in the world. After all, King Kong was able to turn over subway trains and knock airplanes right out of the sky.

Real gorillas are not nearly as scary as King Kong. They do grow large. Some reach six feet and weigh 450 pounds. They also have large teeth and strong muscles. (3)

However, real gorillas do not go around climbing tall buildings or chasing people. Usually they are quiet and keep to themselves. They don't eat people. In fact, they are mainly vegetarians. (4)

Sources
1. *Made in America* by Murray Suid, page 124.
2. *Made in America*, page 124.
3. *Concise Columbia Encyclopedia*, page 329.
4. *Concise Columbia Encyclopedia*, page 329.

Fact-Checking Worksheet

Name of the person checking the facts: _____

Title of the report to be checked: _____

Name of the author of the report: _____

State each fact that you checked and the source (book or person) you used to check it. If the fact is right, mark "OK." If you found an error, give the correct information. If more facts were checked, use the back of this sheet.

Fact 1: _____

Source used to check the fact: _____
( ) OK
Correct information: _____

Fact 2: _____

Source used to check the fact: _____
( ) OK
Correct information: _____

Fact 3: _____

Source used to check the fact: _____
( ) OK
Correct information: _____

Fact 4: _____

Source used to check the fact: _____
( ) OK
Correct information: _____

FIELD TRIPS (WITHOUT A BUS)

Sometimes the most interesting things are right under our noses. Many objects around the school can be used as springboards into science, technology, history, and other important subjects.

DIRECTIONS:
1. Divide the class into groups of four or five students.
2. Have each group scout in and around the building looking for interesting things, such as bricks, concrete, glass windows, fire extinguishers, clocks, the bell, and various plants and trees.
3. Each student in the group researches one item and writes a short speech about it. The presentation might give the history of glass windows, tell how the school bell works, or explain how concrete is made.
4. The team should collaborate on writing and publishing a brochure about the items that will be seen on the field trip.
5. After rehearsing, the group should offer guided field trips to students in the class or to children in lower grades.

EXTENSION:
Students can create self-guided field trips by labeling various items around the school and creating maps telling potential field-trip goers where to find each object. Students could then distribute these maps to different classes, or they could post the maps on bulletin boards.

GIVE A GLOSSARY

Writing definitions requires high-level thinking. In the following activity, that task involves critical reading as well as the use of the dictionary.

DIRECTIONS:

1. Ahead of time, each student writes a solo report on a subject that involves about half a dozen technical words, or more. For example, a report about railroads might include such terms as gauge, grade, locomotive, right of way, terminal, and tie. Each technical word should be underlined. (See sample report on page 35.)

2. Divide the class into pairs and have students exchange their papers.

3. Each student reads the partner's paper and defines the technical words on a piece of scratch paper. The definitions might be figured out from context, by questioning the author, or by consulting a dictionary.

4. After polishing the definitions, the glossary writer arranges them in alphabetical order. (See model glossary on page 36.) The glossary is then attached to the original paper.

5. Add the glossary writer's name to the title page of the report.

EXTENSION:

As an ongoing current events project, students can take turns preparing a "daily definition" of a word found in the newspaper. The definition can be published in the school's daily flyer or posted on a "Word of the Day" bulletin board.

Sample Report with Technical Words

AMAZING DOLPHINS

A dolphin may look like a fish, but it isn't. Though it lives in water, it has no **gills**. It can't breathe underwater the way fish can. It gets **oxygen** from the air, just as people do.

Like people, dolphins are **mammals**. Mother dolphins nurse their babies with milk.

Dolphins breathe through a **dorsal blowhole**. If they're underwater when they breathe out, they create a fountain of water.

These swift swimmers move forward by means of powerful **flukes**, and steer with a **dorsal fin**. They avoid bumping into things by using a kind of **sonar**.

Dolphins are very friendly toward humans and seem to understand language. Many scientists believe that these animals are highly intelligent.

In recent years, thousands of dolphins have been killed in tuna fishing nets. Experts worry that some kinds of dolphins might become **extinct**. This is why many people have been working hard to save these beautiful ocean creatures.

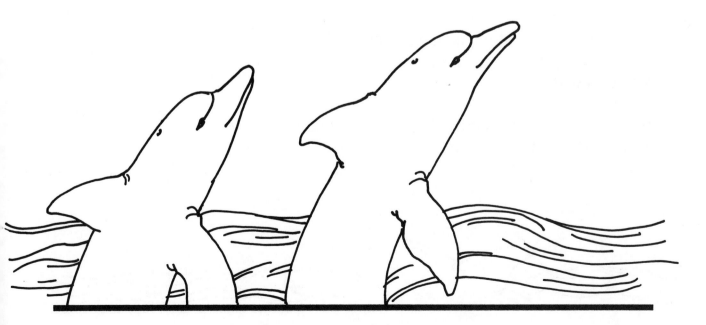

Model Glossary

DOLPHIN WORDS

blowhole: a hole through which dolphins breathe; it is related to the nose in human beings

dorsal: anything that has to do with the back of an animal

extinct: a word used to describe the death of a type of animal or plant; when an animal or plant is extinct, that type of living thing is gone forever

fin: a wing-like part of a dolphin or fish used for swimming and balancing

flukes: the two flat parts of a dolphin's tail

gill: the part of an underwater animal used for breathing; the gills take oxygen out of the water

mammal: a kind of animal that gives birth to its young and that feeds its babies milk; while most mammals live on land, a few, such as dolphins, live in water

oxygen: a gas that animals need in order to live; oxygen is part of the air humans breathe; it is also found in water

sonar: a system of "seeing" by bouncing sound waves off objects

GLOBE AND MAP REPORTS

The following current events activity helps students understand the difference between maps and globes. Students will also become more familiar with different places around the world.

DIRECTIONS:

1. Divide the class into groups of three.
2. Assign each group a time period to cover, for example, the first week of a given month.
3. The group finds an event that occurred during this period in a distant place, such as a forest fire in Central America or a rocket launch in Russia.
4. The students work together to write a brief account of the event, basing their report on information found in newspapers or through other forms of the media. Students also gather facts about their given location, and find it on a map and on a globe.
5. During the presentation, one student describes the event. The other two students use the map and globe to show where the occurrence took place. They also present their information about the location.
6. Students, at their desks, can record the areas where the presented events took place on a world map (page 38). Each month, they can take these maps home to share with family members.

EXTENSION:

Use the same approach to make reports about historical happenings, such as Marco Polo's departure from Venice or the explosion of Vesuvius.

World Map

GRAB BAG COLUMN

The "Grab Bag" trivia column appears in many newspapers. Students can create their own version of this delightful feature for the enjoyment of other students or parents. While sharpening research skills, your researchers might ignite lifelong interests among their readers.

DIRECTIONS:

1. Read aloud a sample "Grab Bag" column found in a newspaper, or write one of your own using fact books.
2. Take a tour of your school or town library's reference section. Introduce students to the many fact books dealing with such subjects as famous firsts, songs, science, sports, inventors, and leaders.
3. Have each student collect three or four unusual facts and then select the most interesting one for publication. (Option: Students can swap their fact lists and have classmates choose.)
4. The chosen facts should be rewritten in the students' own words. The source of the fact should be given at the end of the write-up.
5. Collect one fact from each student and publish the results in the school newspaper, on a hallway bulletin board, or in the home-school flyer.

EXTENSION:

After publishing several columns, have each student choose a favorite fact. The fact should be written on a single piece of paper and illustrated. Collect the pages into a "Grab Bag" book. Copies can be given to the school or local library.

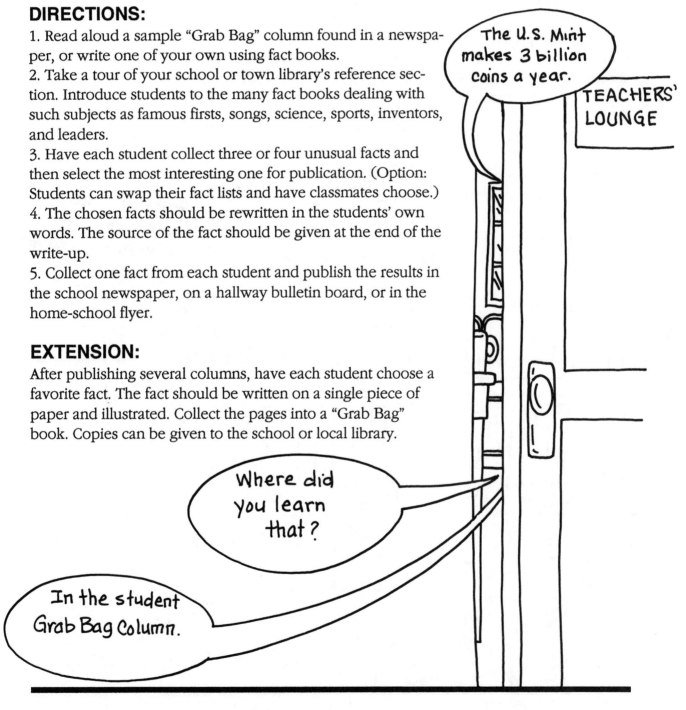

INFORMATION SCAVENGER HUNTS

Many schools sponsor yearly fact scavenger hunts to celebrate researching. When students create the questions, the game becomes even more engrossing.

DIRECTIONS:

1. Divide the class into small groups. Each group chooses a topic. Examples: tornadoes, chipmunks, or ice cream.
2. The groups prepare a question list with five to 10 items from a variety of subject areas. (See sample on page 41.) Writers should simultaneously prepare a list of answers, including the source for each answer.
3. Make copies of the scavenger hunt list for the rest of the class to use. The "scavengers" can work alone or in small groups.
4. After a set period of time, have the scavenger list authors go over the answers with the rest of the class.

EXTENSION:

Share the scavenger hunt sheets with other classes or other schools.

Question three is: "Who was the first woman to win a Nobel Prize?"

Sample Scavenger Hunt List

A SCAVENGER FACT HUNT ABOUT PHOTOGRAPHY AND MOVIES

For each question, give the answer and the source (which book or person gave you the answer).

1. Where does the word "photo" come from?

_____

2. Who invented the daguerreotype?

_____

3. What does the word "camera" mean?

_____

4. In what year did Edwin Land invent the instant-picture camera?

_____

5. How many pictures does a sound motion picture camera take every second?

_____

6. When was the first color photograph taken?

_____

7. What country produces the most cameras each year?

_____

INTRODUCING A SPEAKER

The preface of a book introduces readers to the subject matter they are going to read. Likewise, a person who introduces a speaker gets the audience ready for what they are about to hear.

DIRECTIONS:
1. Have students prepare individual oral reports.
2. Divide the class into pairs.
3. Each student listens to the partner's presentation and asks questions to discover background information. (See "Introduction Planner" on page 43.)
4. Partners write introductions for each other.
5. Each student then introduces the partner's presentation to the class.

EXTENSION:
Students can use the same procedure for introducing classroom guests.

Mandy is our geography expert of the week. She'll be talking about Sydney, Australia, where one of her cousins lives.

Introduction Planner

These steps can help you get ready to introduce a speaker to an audience. If you need more space, use the back or another sheet of paper.

Step 1. Talk to the speaker in order to gather the facts you'll need to write the introduction.

( ) Speaker's name:_____
If the name is unusual, write it as it sounds. For example, the name "Suid" rhymes with "fluid."

( ) Title of the speech:_____

_____

( ) Subject of the speech:_____

_____

( ) How did the speaker get interested in this topic?_____

_____

( ) How did the speaker learn about the subject?_____

_____

( ) Why should listeners be interested in the subject?____

_____

Step 2. Write your introduction using some or all of the information you gathered.

Step 3. Show your introduction to the speaker. Make sure it fits in with his or her speech.

Step 4. Rehearse the introduction as you would any speech.

JIGSAW PANELS

Every piece in a jigsaw puzzle helps form the picture. In the same way, each member of a "jigsaw" panel makes a contribution to the whole report.

DIRECTIONS:

1. Prepare a list of topics about things which have several parts. For example, an airplane has wings, flaps, engine, a tail, and a body. (See page 45 for other jigsaw topics.)
2. Divide the class into groups.
3. Have each group choose a topic. The group should have the same number of students as the topic has parts, plus one extra member who will act as spokesperson.
4. Each student will investigate and write a short speech on one part of the thing, with the spokesperson gathering overview material.
5. Students rehearse and then—possibly wearing costumes—present what they learned to the rest of the class. After delivering their set lines, group members, still in character, might field questions.

EXTENSION:

Use the same format to report on step-by-step processes. For example, digestion involves chewing the food, mixing the food with saliva, sending the food to the stomach where it's churned with digestive juices, and moving the food through the intestines.

Next, we'll hear how Ear is connected to Nose.

Jigsaw Topics

baseball glove: fingers, heel, pocket, webbing

blimp: engine, envelope, gondola, horizontal fin, landing wheel, mooring attachment, night sign

business letter: body, closing, greeting, inside address, return address

camera: body, film, lens, shutter, shutter release, viewfinder

cat's head: ears, eyes, forehead, lips, nose leather, whiskers

coin: edge, field, inscription, motto, portrait

computer: CPU, keyboard, monitor, mouse, software

dictionary entry: definitions, etymology, pronunciation key

feather: quill, shaft, vane

fire hydrant: barrel (standpipe), bonnet, chain cap, nose nozzle cap, operating nut

head: ears, eyes, mouth, nose, chin, hair

igloo: air hole, king block, snow blocks, tunnel (tossut)

light bulb: filament, globe, socket

lock: cylinder, key, tumblers

mouth: lips, palate, teeth, tongue

mushroom: cap, gills, mycelium ring, stem

pay phone: coin box, coin slot, cord, handset, push-buttons, switch hook

pencil: body, eraser, lead (graphite)

sailboat: boom, keel, mainsail, mast, masthead, rudder

shoe: eyelets, heel, sole, tongue, upper

tepee: cover, door, ear, lodge poles, outside pole (flap pole), smoke flap

zipper: bottom stop, slide, teeth

LEARNING HANG-UPS

This activity allows the students to become teachers. They will discover the thrill of sharing information with classmates or others in the school. (You may even instill a lifelong interest in teaching among some of your students.)

DIRECTIONS:

1. To familiarize students with the forms and functions of bulletin boards, hand out and discuss the "Bulletin Board Primer" (page 47) and "Bulletin Board Models" (pages 48 and 49).
2. Divide the class into small groups and have each group prepare a small bulletin board display on a subject that you've been studying. If there isn't sufficient bulletin board space in your room or in nearby hallways to present all of the work at once, students can take turns displaying their efforts.

EXTENSION:

Have students explore other hang-up formats, such as window hangings, door decorations, sandwich boards, and outside displays. See the gallery on page 50.

Reuse what you can.
Eliminate waste.
Choose products wisely.
Yell against pollution.
Clean up the planet.
Leave resources for the future.
Enjoy a healthier life.

Bulletin Board Primer

1. Pick a subject.

2. Decide what the bulletin board will focus on and write a title.

3. Find the place where the bulletin board will be. Measure the area.

4. Sketch what the board will look like. List the materials you will use.

5. Collect the materials.

6. Write all the words for the board.

7. After polishing the words, print them neatly by hand or use a computer.

8. Put the board together.

9. Ask a few people if they can suggest a way to make the board better.

Bulletin Board Models

Background Information Page

Headline

Boards can be used to show art work, poems, stories, photographs or other creations.

Names of people who made the board

Photo

Artifact

Boards can be used to tell a story or report on an event.

Bulletin Board Models

Boards can be used to teach skills.

Boards can be used to ask people to take a certain action.

LIVING PUPPETS

Actions can speak louder than words. But in the following project, actions speak *with* words.

DIRECTIONS:

1. Each student chooses a topic that involves a demonstration, for example, how to operate a computer or how to administer the Heimlich maneuver to a choking victim. (See page 52 for more examples.)
2. After researching the topic, the student creates a script that involves one or more classmates who will act as "puppets" during the demonstration.
3. The speaker teaches the student "puppets" their parts.
4. During the presentation to the class, the speaker reads or recites the script as the "puppets" go through their motions.

EXTENSION:

Videotape the show to share with other classes and people at home.

Topics to Demonstrate

book making

calling 911 to report an emergency

casting a fishing line

doing multiplication

drawing a cartoon

eating spaghetti

eating with chopsticks

fly casting

flying a kite

kneading bread dough

knitting

looking up a word in a dictionary

making a clay pot

making a paper airplane

patching an inner tube

planting a window box

playing a guitar or other musical instrument

putting on a puppet show

repairing a torn page in a book

setting up a simple electric circuit

sewing on a button

shooting a free throw

taking a photograph

taking one's temperature

threading a needle

tying a bow tie or regular tie

typewriting

using elegant table manners

using sign language for the deaf

walking on stilts

weaving a mat or basket

weighing something on a balance scale

wrapping a package

MADE FOR EACH OTHER

Paired subjects heard in familiar phrases ("thunder and lightning") can serve as starting points for two-person reports. Each partner presents one of the subjects. Together, the students discuss how the topics relate.

DIRECTIONS:

1. Present a model report to the class to help students understand what is expected of them. (See page 54.)
2. Divide the class into pairs.
3. Assign each team a two-part subject. Examples include: bees and flowers, bow and arrow, bread and butter, cats and dogs, heads and tails (of a coin), horse and carriage, knife and fork, lock and key, needle and thread, rice and beans, shoes and socks, soap and water, spoke and wheel, sun and moon.
4. Each partner researches and writes a brief report about one subject.
5. Together, the partners prepare material on how the items fit together. For example, in talking about cats and dogs, partners might create a Venn diagram showing how these animals are alike and different.
6. Partners present their reports to the class.

EXTENSION:

Have students write and present puppet dialogues in which personifications of their topics talk about themselves.

Sample Dialogue

FLOWERS AND BEES

Student 1

Today, we'll be talking about bees . . .

Student 2

. . . and flowers.

Student 1

Bees are insects. When people think of bees, they usually first think about the stinger. But a more important part is the bee's large hind feet. These are used for gathering pollen and nectar.

Student 2

The flower is the part of a plant that makes seeds, which may grow into new plants. The flower is made up of four kinds of leaves. The outer leaves, called sepals, are green. The colorful leaves are called petals. In the middle of the petals are the stamens, which contain pollen. In the center of the stamens is the pistil. It contains eggs which are called ovules. The eggs become seeds when they come into contact with pollen. This is called pollination. Pollination usually works best when eggs are pollinated with pollen from other plants.

Student 1

That's where bees come in. As a bee moves from one flower to another, it carries pollen with it on its legs. Sometimes a few grains of pollen will rub off. If this pollen causes a seed to form, it's called cross-pollination.

Student 2

Cross-pollination is so important, farmers may spend a lot of money buying bees.

MANY-SIDED REPORTS

The folk tale "Six Blind Men and the Elephant" shows the risk of taking a narrow view of a subject. The following activity helps students learn to see the big picture.

DIRECTIONS:

1. Divide the class into groups.
2. Have each group pick a topic that can be looked at from several perspectives. Example: the ocean has very different meanings for surfers, deep-sea divers, commercial fishing operators, submarine crews, ship captains, oil explorers, garbage dumpers, and fish. (See page 56 for more multifaceted subjects.)
3. Each group member researches the topic from one point of view.
4. Have each group share what they learn among themselves and, later, with the whole class.

EXTENSION:

Assign solo reports in which students treat a subject from several perspectives.

Many-Sided Subjects

SUBJECT	WAYS TO LOOK AT IT
automobile	concert hall, killer, polluter, shelter, sporting equipment, transportation machine
bee	dancer, health hazard, home builder, honey maker, pollen spreader
clothing	protection against weather, sign of wealth, sign of membership in a group (uniform), art form (designer clothes)
computer	adding machine, game player, scientific tool, writing machine
food	fuel, health hazard, product to sell
moon	base for space travel, place to live, source of raw materials
rocket	scientific tool (for exploring the atmosphere), transportation machine, weapon
school	place to learn, place to meet friends, place to prepare for a job
sunlight	by-product of fusion power, energy source, health hazard
television	baby-sitter, electronic marvel, entertainer, friend, furniture, sales person, store (shopping channel), teacher (educational programs), time waster
tree	air conditioner, flood controller, food maker, habitat, jungle gym, wood maker
water	raw material for growing things, cleaning product, material for entertainment (in swimming pool), material for fighting fires, means for cooking things (boiling eggs)

MAP SANDWICHES

Cartographers create complex maps layer by layer: different transparencies carry different types of information. Students can create this kind of map "sandwich" for use in map presentations.

DIRECTIONS:

1. Using different kinds of maps, review the types of information that a map may give. (See page 58 for a list of items that can be mapped.)
2. Divide the class into groups. Each group will choose a place to map, for example, a city or a country.
3. Give each student an outline map of the area. (Use one of the duplicatable map masters starting on page 59.)
4. All students should draw the outline of the place onto a blank transparency.
5. Assign each student a type of data to map. For example, one student might handle streets while a partner takes responsibility for railroads.
6. With the help of an atlas or other reference, each student maps the information onto the blank transparency, using a different-color washable-ink felt-tip pen. The data may take the form of lines, symbols, and words.
7. Students present their findings to the class by projecting and discussing each transparency separately, then sandwich them together to make a composite map.

EXTENSION:

Students can use the same technique to report on the body's various internal organs.

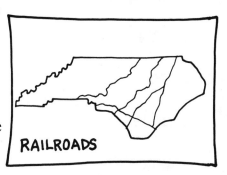

CITIES

RAILROADS

MOUNTAINS, LAKES, AND RIVERS

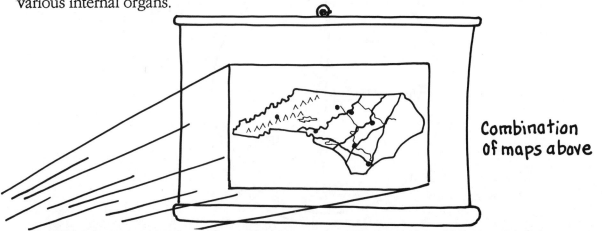

Combination of maps above

Information That Can Appear on a Map

airline routes

airports

automobile highways

bays

buildings (on local maps)

canals

cities

counties

countries

dams

deserts

forests

gulfs

highways

islands

lakes

lines of latitude

lines of longitude

minerals (deposits of coal, etc.)

mountains

oceans

parks

railways

rivers

streets

symbols (indicating capital cities, compass points, rainfall, temperature, etc.)

valleys

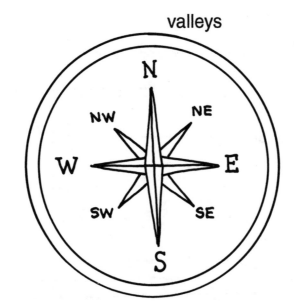

Map Master: Africa

Map Master: Asia

Map Master: Australia

Map Master: Europe

Map Master: North America

Map Master: South America

MODEL THINKING

Scientists, architects, and other thinkers build models to make the abstract real, and to see old things in new ways. Model-making also gives practice in turning words and pictures into three-dimensional objects. This kind of translating is a high-level thinking skill.

DIRECTIONS:

1. Divide the class into model-making groups.
2. Each group chooses an object to represent as a three-dimensional model, for example, the human heart or a moon crater. (See page 66 for more objects to model.)
3. The group researches the topic, collecting as much visual information as they can about it.
4. After deciding on the model's size, and making sketches, the group should collect materials for the construction. They might use cardboard, cloth, string, tin cans, egg cartons, and other on-hand items. The chief ingredient will be their imagination.
5. When the model is completed, the group writes an explanation to be posted next to it, or a script to be read aloud by a student docent.

EXTENSION:

As a whole-class project, build a walk-through museum that gives visitors an inside look at an object, such as the human ear. A museum in Philadelphia boasts a giant walk-through heart where visitors listen to a heartbeat that sounds something like a motorcycle engine revving!

Objects to Model

ball point pen

brain

building (Washington Monument, London Bridge, the Roman Coliseum, etc.)

cell (blood cell, onion cell, etc.)

clock

cylinder of a gasoline engine

ear

egg

electric motor

eye

faucet

flower

heart

intestine

light bulb

light switch

lock

mouth

music box

popcorn

spaceship

spider web

stomach

trumpet (or other musical instrument)

vacuum cleaner

whistle

zipper

Popcorn Kernel

OBJECT INTERVIEWS

The following activity shows how report makers can bring to life subjects ranging from single-celled animals to the moon.

DIRECTIONS:

1. Divide the class into pairs.
2. Each pair chooses an object on which to report, for example, the brain. (See page 68 for more objects.)
3. The students research their subject, and then write a script in which the object is interviewed.
4. The team then creates a costume that represents the object. It should be big enough for one of the partners to wear or get inside.
5. During the report, one student interviews the object.

EXTENSION:

Have two objects carry on a conversation. For example, the full moon could chat with a crescent moon about the phases they go through. Or a computer could argue with a pencil about which is the better instrument for writing.

Objects to Interview

baseball, football, or other piece of sporting equipment

carrot or other vegetable

compact disc

computer

consonant or vowel

diamond or other mineral

dinosaur or other animal

dollar bill

egg

Eiffel Tower or any famous building

fork, knife, or spoon

hammer or any other building tool

hat, shoe, or other article of clothing

heart, eye, or other body part

letter of the alphabet

milk carton

minus, plus, or other mathematical symbol

moon or other celestial object

penny or other coin

pine tree or pine cone

rainbow

snowflake

state or nation (map outline)

telephone

telescope

violin or other musical instrument

vitamin pill

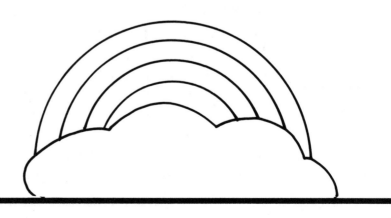

PARAPHRASING PARTNERS

Writing ideas in one's own words is a key research skill which exercises high-level thinking. The following activity teaches the strategy of not looking at the original material while paraphrasing. This approach helps solve the problem of mindless copying.

DIRECTIONS:

1. Have each student find or write a short nonfiction piece containing two or more paragraphs.
2. Divide the class into pairs.
3. One member of each pair reads aloud the first paragraph of his or her piece while the partner listens.
4. The listening partner then writes down the ideas without trying to capture the exact words.
5. The reader continues, paragraph by paragraph until the passage has been completed. Then the partners compare the new version with the original, to make sure key ideas were accurately handled.
6. Swap roles, with the student who paraphrased now reading, while the former reader does the paraphrasing.

EXTENSION:

Students practice the process on their own by reading a text and writing down three or four key words for each paragraph. The original material is put aside, and students then "reconstitute" the piece using only their notes.

The yo-yo is one of the world's oldest toys. A 2500-year-old vase from Greece shows a boy playing with a yo-yo.

The yo-yo is a very old toy. Thousands of years ago children in Greece played with yo-yos. We know this because of pictures on old vases.

PASS-IT-ON LEARNING

Scientists, inventors, and other creative workers often build on the achievements of those who came before them. Your current students can experience this across-the-years cooperation by beginning projects future students will continue.

DIRECTIONS:

1. Begin an open-ended research project that will involve the entire class. For example, you might study weather patterns throughout the year, measuring precipitation, temperature, cloud patterns, and so on. Younger students can help fill out a class calendar, describing the weather for each day ("Today was cloudy, windy, and cool").
2. At the end of the year, publish the findings in one or more class books, using ring binders so that new data can be added later on. Be sure to date all reports.
3. When the new school year begins, introduce the ongoing project. Share the work of the earlier student researchers.
4. Assign new students tasks for carrying on the research.

EXTENSION:

Have students report on inventions or discoveries that involved people at different times in history, for example, engineers who worked at different times to develop the airplane or the rocket.

PEN PAL REPORTS

Freud and Einstein once exchanged a series of letters that dealt with the question, "Why is there war?" This give-and-take method of learning brought insights to those geniuses, and it can do the same for your students.

DIRECTIONS:
1. Each student chooses and investigates a topic such as the greenhouse effect or the invention of jazz.
2. Students write "To Whom It May Concern" letters, telling what they learned. These letters might end in a question that could lead to further research.
3. Students exchange letters at random with classmates.
4. Each student uses the letter received as a starting point for finding out something else about the topic.
5. This new information is written in another letter and sent back to the original writer. (See the example on page 72.)
6. Continue the correspondence a few more times, then bind each set of letters into a booklet.

EXTENSION:
Have students, working alone or in small groups, locate an out-of-school expert to correspond with about a topic the expert is familiar with. For example, students interested in the oceans might exchange letters with a scuba diver or a sailor.

Here's a letter from a class that's studying leadership. I think I can give them some help.

Sample Pen-Pal Report

To Whom It May Concern,

I have been learning about the Frisbee. This terrific toy was invented by Walter Morrison in the 1940s. He got the idea after tossing pie tins and coffee-can lids when he was a kid.

In the late 1940s, he carved his first model out of a kind of plastic called "tenite." When he got the shape he wanted, he bought a molding machine and went into business. Later, a big company bought Morrison's invention and changed the name to Frisbee. I'd like to find out more about this toy. Can you tell me anything?

Peter

Dear Peter,

I enjoyed reading your letter about Frisbees. Maybe you'll be interested in how to train a dog to catch one of these things. The first thing is to let your pet play with the Frisbee. Then, play a game of tug of war with you holding the Frisbee in your hand, and the dog holding it in his mouth.

Then roll the disk on the ground and see if the dog will run after it and catch it. If it does, give a reward.

Next, try tossing the Frisbee a few inches from your hand to the dog's mouth. When he can catch it, step back a little and keep increasing the distance.

Let me know how this works.

Nancy

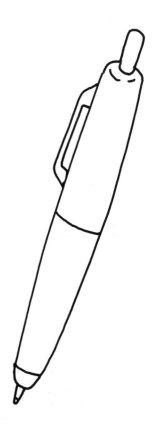

PHONY PHONE-IN RADIO

A tape-recorded "talk radio" program gives students practice in defending their opinions with facts.

DIRECTIONS:

1. Divide the class into groups of five or six. One student will play the host, the rest will be callers.

2. The students choose a topic on which to report. For best results, the topic ought to inspire pro and con opinions, for example, "Should we spend money building a space station?" (See page 74 for more topics.)

3. After choosing either the pro or con side, each student researches the topic.

4. Meet with students individually to discuss the information they have discovered. This may make them more comfortable about presenting their views to the rest of the class.

5. When ready to produce the program, students sit around a tape recorder. The host begins by greeting listeners and bringing up the topic. Then the host interacts with "callers," some of whom can pretend to be using cellular car phones. These conversations can be improvised or scripted.

6. To add realism, the program can be interrupted by reporters who read news briefs, commercials, and traffic reports.

7. Play the tape for the whole class to enjoy.

EXTENSION:

Arrange for the class to visit a radio station while a talk show is in progress. Or invite a talk-show host to visit your classroom to discuss this type of programming.

Talk-Radio Topics

animal rights: Should animals be used for medical research?

language: Should the country have a single official language?

metrics: Should the metric system be used for all measurements?

population: Is the world getting overpopulated?

radiation: Is radiated food safe?

schools: Should the school year be increased in length?

space travel: Should we invest money in a space station and in trips to the planets?

television: Should children's television viewing be limited?

PRESS CONFERENCES

Asking questions is a powerful way to learn about a subject. The following activity offers practice in sharpening the reporter's skills.

DIRECTIONS:

1. Divide the class into small groups.
2. Each group chooses a topic with multiple parts.
For example, the study of clouds includes nimbus clouds, cirrus clouds, and cumulus clouds. The topic of wind includes hurricanes, cyclones, and blizzards. (See page 76 for other topics.)
3. Each member of the group investigates one part of the topic.
4. When the group has finished investigating, it appears before the rest of the class. After each member makes a brief presentation, the chairperson invites questions from classmates, who take on the role of reporters.
5. At the end of the presentation, reporters write their stories, which are gathered into a newspaper "extra."

EXTENSION:

Arrange for all sorts of experts from the school or town community to face your classroom press corps. These real-world specialists might include doctors, plumbers, architects, gardeners, artists, and politicians. Publish a transcript of each encounter in a group-written article for the school or town newspaper.

PRESS CORPS

Press Conference Topics

baseball positions: first base, second base, shortstop, catcher, etc.

bodies of water: bays, gulfs, lakes, oceans, rivers, seas

colors: primary or rainbow colors

Dewey Decimal categories

digestive system: mouth, stomach, small intestine, large intestine

family relationships: cousin, uncle, grandparent, etc.

geological formations: mountain, plateau, valley, etc.

geo-political categories: city, county, state, nation

mathematical operations: addition, subtraction, multiplication, division

measurements: meter, liter, kilogram

musical notations: clef, sharp, flat, musical note, tempo

parts of the eye: cornea, iris, pupil, etc.

planets: Jupiter, Venus, etc.

punctuation marks: comma, dash, exclamation point, period, quotation marks, etc.

seasons

senses: hearing, seeing, tasting, smelling, touching

tastes: sweet, sour, bitter, salty

teeth: molars, bicuspids, etc.

tree parts: roots, trunk, branches, leaves

vitamins: A, B, C, D, E, etc.

words: antonyms, homonyms, synonyms

Press Conference Topics
baseball positions
bodies of water
colors

PUPPET PRESENTATIONS

While most puppets resemble human beings, puppetry can also be used to personify inanimate objects and abstractions, such as numbers and symbols.

DIRECTIONS:

1. Divide the class into small groups.
2. Each group chooses a subject with two or more related items (for example, the capital and lower-case forms of a letter), or a single object that has several parts (for example, an eyeball or a tree).
3. One group member collects general information, such as facts about the whole eye. Others zero in on one part, for example, the iris or the cornea.
4. Students prepare brief speeches about their areas of expertise. They might want to script conversations among the parts. Example: in a presentation about a tree, the root and the trunk might discuss how they work together to bring nutrients to the leaves.
5. Students then create puppets. In a report on a tree, there might be an overall tree puppet, a root puppet, a trunk puppet, a branch puppet, a leaf puppet, and a fruit puppet, all made of cardboard, papier-mache, or other readily available materials.
6. After rehearsing their presentations, groups present their reports to the entire class.

EXTENSION:

Students can present their shows as TV programs, à la "Sesame Street."

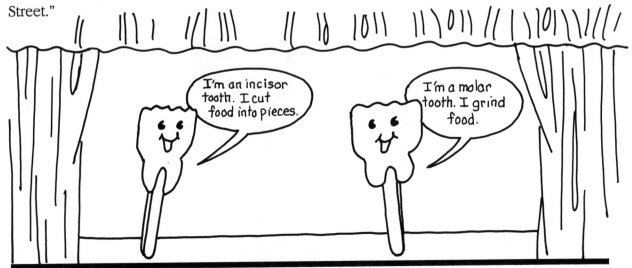

QUESTION SWAPPING

Good questions are often the starting point for breakthroughs in science, invention, and the arts.

DIRECTIONS:

1. Each student chooses a topic and then writes as many questions as possible about it. For example, the topic "house fly" might inspire such questions as:
- How fast can a fly fly?
- How long does a fly live?
- Can a fly bite?
- Are flies really dirty?
- Do flies sleep at night?
- How do flies walk on walls and ceilings?
- How do flies eat?
- Why do flies "buzz"?

2. Students swap their question lists with a partner, who does research to answer the questions.

3. Reporters then share the answers with the original questioner and with the entire class.

EXTENSION:

Set up a research service in which your students answer questions posed by children in lower grades. Use the material in an "Answer Column" in the school newspaper.

QUIZ SHOWS

Preparing questions for a quiz show can stretch the mind even more than the actual contest can. The following activity has a bonus: the fun of trying to "stump the teacher."

DIRECTIONS:

1. Ahead of time, assemble two teams of adults from among the faculty and staff.
2. Have the class decide on the format of the game: teams can take turns answering questions, or each team can have a noise maker to "ring." Also, the class can make prizes for the winning team and for the "runner up" group.
3. Divide the class into small groups. Each group researches a single topic and writes five to 10 questions. Questions should take the form of true/false, multiple choice, or "short answer" (name, date, or number). Each question and the source for the answer (title of book or magazine plus page number) should be written on a note card.
4. During the show, students take turns firing questions at the two teams. A panel of scorekeepers can check the answers and total the results.

EXTENSION:

Create a fantasy quiz show in which students, playing famous people, answer questions designed for the celebrities. For example, if Columbus were one of the contestants, there might be a question about the name of his three ships.

RADIO NEWS PROGRAMS

Putting on a tape-recorded "radio" news program builds interest in current events. It also sharpens oral reading skills.

DIRECTIONS:

1. As a class, listen to a radio news broadcast that covers a variety of topics: local, national, international, sports, movies, and so on. Discuss the format of the overall broadcast and each segment within it.

2. Have the class choose call letters for the station and set up a "radio news studio" in one corner of the classroom.

3. Form several production "units" of about five or six students. Each group member will report on a different kind of news.

4. Have the groups take turns writing and recording five-minute news programs for "broadcast" to the class. Material can be gathered by rewriting items found in a local newspaper and by interviewing students and teachers. (See a sample script on page 81.)

EXTENSION:

Create fact-based (but imaginary) news programs that might have been broadcast at momentous times in history, for example, the day Mexico won its independence. Or have students invent news shows of the future, for example, on the day contact is made with beings from another planet.

Sample Radio News Script

Reporter 1
W-R-L-D news is on the air. Our top story is that a jet skidded off a New York runway. The Chicago-bound plane was about to take off when a warning light came on. The pilot then shut down the engines. None of the 292 passengers was seriously hurt. Most of the plane burned up after the passengers slid down emergency chutes.

Reporter 2
In local news, cat owners are complaining about a new law that says cats must be kept on leashes. The cat lovers claim that cats need their freedom.

Reporter 3
There's big news in space. For the first time, astronauts from four different countries rode a shuttle into orbit. The astronauts come from the U.S., Canada, Russia, and Italy. Experts say that teamwork is important because future space missions may cost more than any one country can afford. Scientists are talking about a Mars trip that will bring together astronauts from 10 nations.

Reporter 4
The local weather has been unusually warm for this late in the year. The high temperature yesterday was 82 degrees. The low was 67. Today may be two degrees hotter.

Reporter 5
The sports front was quiet today. Things will pick up tomorrow with the first game of the World Series.

Reporter 1
And that's the news for the day. Have a safe afternoon. W-R-L-D is off the air.

RALLY REPORTS

Street theater can be a dramatic way to educate as well as entertain. Students can take their messages to the playground or even (with permission) the lunchroom.

DIRECTIONS:

1. Choose a topic that the class has been studying, for example, recycling. (See page 83 for more topics.)
2. Divide the class into small groups.
3. Each group should come up with some sort of movable display that conveys information about the topic. Displays can take many forms, including banners, wagon-mounted floats, sandwich boards, costumes, and picket signs.
4. Students, individually or in small groups, should write and rehearse chants, speeches, and song lyrics that can be sung to familiar tunes.
5. A committee of students should meet with the principal to arrange a time and place for the rally.
6. Publicize the rally by putting up posters and writing announcements for the school's daily flyer. You might also alert the town's newspapers and TV stations.
7. Put on the rally.

EXTENSION:

Videotape the rally to share with parents and with students in other schools.

Fascinating Dinosaur Facts

Come to the Dinosaur Rally at lunch

Rally Topics

the arts

bicycle safety

citizenship

cleanliness

cultural awareness

drug education

environment

geography

grade level report (e.g., what sixth grade is all about)

home safety

library (all the things that you can find there)

literacy (e.g., the benefits of reading)

manners

nutrition

pet care

physical fitness

predicting the future

recycling

tolerance

vocational awareness

READING LISTS

Bibliographies are a valuable educational tool. They help readers learn about subjects in depth. The following activity aims to help students feel comfortable about using reading lists by first creating their own.

DIRECTIONS:

1. Each student writes a short report based on personal knowledge, for example, "My Aunt, the Veterinarian." The piece should include many details, such as why the aunt chose her field, what school she attended, the courses she took, and what she does during a typical day. (See page 85 for more topics.)
2. Students swap papers with partners.
3. Each student lists one or more topics found in—or related to—the report. For example, in a biography of a letter carrier, one topic might be the history of the post office. Another might be services provided by the government.
4. In the library, students locate several books that deal with the topics in the partner's paper.
5. After reading these resources, or at least looking over their contents pages and introductions, students prepare a short reading list to accompany the partner's paper. For a model, use the reading list on page 125 of this book.
6. Students attach the reading lists to the partners' papers, and return the reports to the authors.

EXTENSION:

Try the same activity starting with fiction or poetry. For example, a reading list accompanying a fantasy story about a trip to Mars might feature factual books about rockets, the planets, and space travel.

Topics for Personalized Reports

animals:
- Living with a Tarantula
- Milking a Cow

chores:
- Painting Our Garage
- Weeding a Garden

emergencies:
- How a Smoke Alarm Saved Our Neighbors
- What to Do in an Earthquake

experiences:
- My Appendectomy
- Moving to a New City

history:
- My Great-grandmother's Life in Russia
- What Happened to My Neighbor in the War

hobbies:
- Collecting Baseball Cards
- Painting with Watercolors

jobs:
- My Mom's Life as a Real Estate Agent
- My Cousin Is a Used Car Salesman

observations:
- A Car Crash on My Street
- The Day the Sewers Flooded

skills:
- Playing the Tuba
- Flying a Kite

trips:
- Our Family's Visit to Niagara Falls
- They Speak French in Montreal

REENACTMENTS

Drama is a powerful device for making history less abstract. In the following activity, students use the "you are there" strategy for bringing past events to life.

DIRECTIONS:

1. Divide the class into groups.
2. Help each group choose an historical event, such as the signing of the Declaration of Independence. (See page 87 for more examples.)
3. Students should research their event. In addition to collecting facts, this might include making sketches of how things looked.
4. All information should be brought together in a script.
5. After rehearsing the script, students present the event for the entire class.

EXTENSION:

As an ongoing current events project, reenact stories from the newspaper.

Events to Reenact

Note: When an event involves a large object such as the *Titanic*, huge props aren't needed. Actors can reenact the occurrence by playing the role of an eyewitness who observes the thing offstage: "Look, the ship's bow is going down!"

battle of Lexington

Benjamin Franklin's lightning experiment using a kite

Boston Tea Party

Columbus' arrival in the "new" world

crash of the *Hindenberg*

dedication of the Eiffel Tower

dedication of the Statue of Liberty

discovery of penicillin

first atom bomb explosion

first balloon flight

first flight of the Wright brothers

first moon landing by Apollo astronauts

first telephone call

first telegraph message

opening of the Panama Canal

Pilgrims landing at Plymouth Rock

RESEARCH RIDDLE BOOK

The word "riddle" has the same root as the word "read." The connection is apt given the following activity, which involves basing riddles on library research. The end product is a cooperatively produced book.

DIRECTIONS:

1. Each student gathers facts about a different subject. One riddler might research the Ferris wheel, another the Grand Canyon. (See page 89 for additional riddle subjects.)

2. The facts are listed on one side of a piece of paper, working from the most obscure to the most obvious. For example:

- This thing was invented in 1829.
- It contains metal reeds.
- It has buttons and keys.
- It uses air.
- Its name means "to be in tune."
- Its user pushes and pulls on it.
- It makes music.

3. The writer prints the riddle's answer on the back of the paper ("It's an accordion!") and, optionally, draws a picture of the subject.

4. All the pages are bound into a class book of riddles. Copies can be donated to the school and town libraries.

EXTENSION:

Publish one riddle in the daily flyer or broadcast it over the PA system as part of morning announcements.

Today's Riddle is by Sara
1. It started with the Egyptians.
2. The Phoencian's worked on it.
3. Later, the Greeks borrowed the idea.
4. The Romans learned it from the Greeks.
5. We use it every day in this school.
6. It has 26 parts.
7. It's used in writing and reading.

Riddle Subjects

alphabet

ball point pen

basketball

bicycle

braces for teeth

Braille

chocolate

computer

eyeglasses

flute

gasoline

gold

Gulf of Mexico

helicopter

kindergarten

meter

microwave oven

neon sign

Panama Canal

radio

rock 'n roll

rodeo

roller coaster

Saint Lawrence Seaway

sandwich

snowflake

submarine

subway

tea bag

umbrella

videotape recorder

virus

zipper

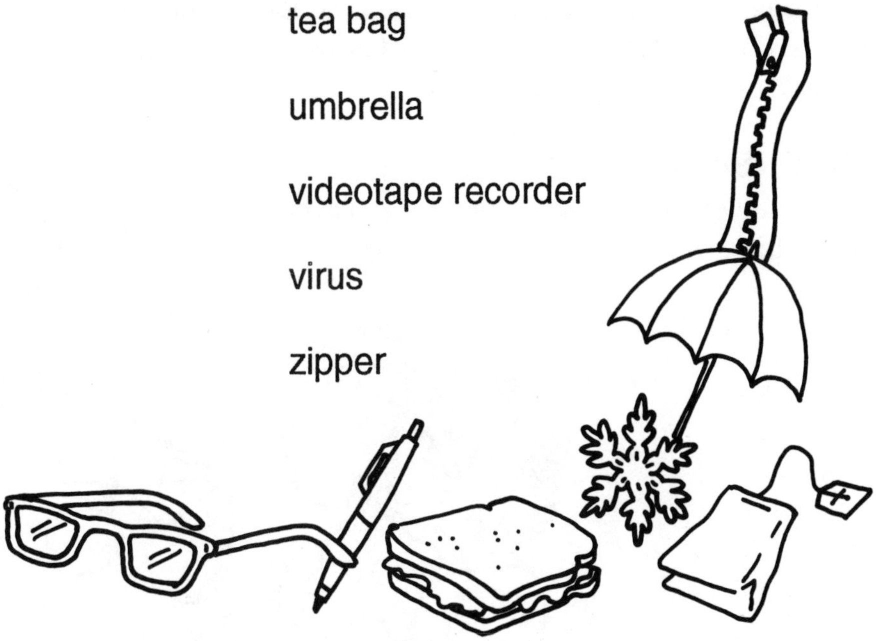

SCIENCE FAIR

The traditional science fair is a competition with winners and losers. In this version, the single goal is sharing knowledge that the students have acquired in their science studies. The experience may inspire some students to participate in more traditional science fairs.

DIRECTIONS:

1. Divide the class into small groups.
2. Each group chooses a topic or process that can be demonstrated in a few minutes. Examples include:
   - how a flashlight works
   - taking one's temperature
   - using a microscope
   - identifying poison ivy
   - making paper
   - taking one's pulse
   - how a stethoscope works and what a doctor hears through it
3. Students gather or create things they'll need for their demonstrations. They then rehearse their presentations, getting feedback from classmates in other groups.
4. Choose a time and place for the fair and have students publicize the event.
5. During the fair, students will repeat their demonstrations several times. Later, help them evaluate the program, and discuss how future fairs might be improved.

EXTENSION:

Create a television science program, which can be circulated to other classes and to homes via videotape.

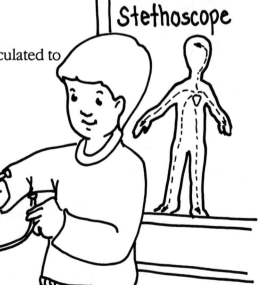

How To Use A Stethoscope

SCIENTIFIC TEAMWORK

Scientific discoveries are accepted only after a researcher's findings are confirmed by other investigators. This proven method of truth seeking can be practiced easily in the classroom.

DIRECTIONS:

1. Set up an observation center with a magnifying glass, a measuring stick with fine calibrations, postage or scientific scale, microscope, or other observation aids.
2. Put an object to observe in the center, for example, a golf ball. (See page 92 for more possibilities.)
3. Divide the class into groups and have them go to the center at different times. Give each student an observation form to complete (page 93). Stress the importance of looking for specialized information. For example, an important fact about a golf ball is how many dimples (depressions) cover its surface. Determining such information is similar to counting or estimating the number of craters on the moon.
4. Have students in each group summarize their findings, noting areas of agreement and disagreement.
5. After observations have been made, have the different groups compare their findings. If discrepancies are detected, the teacher or a group can reexamine the object while the entire class watches.

EXTENSION:

On a bulletin board, students publish results of independent observations, for example, an estimate of the number of leaves on a tree in front of the school. Passers-by can be invited to submit their own observations.

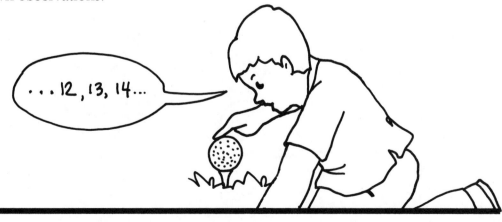

Objects to Observe

baseball

bone from a chicken or other animal

butterfly (mounted)

coin (penny, nickel, etc.)

dollar bill (photocopy)

drinking straw

fabric square

feather

fruit (orange, banana, etc.), either whole or sliced

hair (human or animal)

house key

leaf

model (car, airplane, animal, etc.)

newspaper front page

paper plate

phonograph disk (old long-playing record)

plastic cup

postage stamp

prepared microscope slide—of a cell, a crystal, or other hard-to-see object

seashell

tin of food (filled, with label removed)

videocassette

wood piece showing the grain

yarn

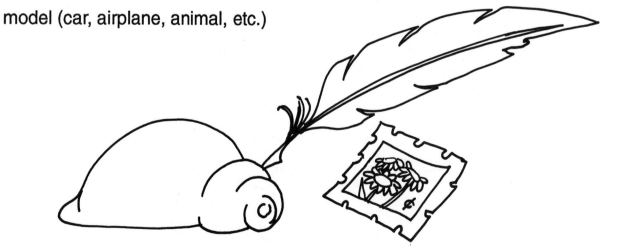

Observation Form

Name of observer: _____

Date: _____ Place of observation: _____

Object observed: _____

Note: Skip points that don't fit the object.

1. Length of object: _____

2. Width of object: _____

3. Weight of object: _____

4. Color or colors of object: _____

5. List words, symbols, or other marks (if the object is covered with words, sum up what they say):

_____

6. Describe unusual parts of the object. When possible, give numbers, for example, "The object has 25 tiny bumps."

_____

7. Tell how the object feels (smooth, slippery, etc.): _____

_____

8. Describe how the object smells: _____

9. Describe any sounds the object makes: _____

10. On the back or another sheet of paper, draw one or more views of the object. Label the important parts.

SPEAKERS BUREAU

Every student is a fountain of knowledge. By creating a speakers bureau that taps this wisdom, you'll enrich the whole school while building your students' self-esteem.

DIRECTIONS:

1. Explain that a speakers bureau is a group of people who share what they know by giving speeches and demonstrations requested by an audience.
2. Conduct a survey of what your students know. You might start by having them fill out the "What I Know" sheet on page 95.
3. Organize the students' knowledge alphabetically, either using note cards or a computer.
4. Have students publicize their knowledge-sharing service by creating bulletin boards, flyers, and sample presentations to give at an assembly.
5. Whenever a request is made for a speaker, send along an assistant who can give an introduction and handle materials.

EXTENSION:

Preserve knowledge for future students by videotaping the presentations.

What I Know

Name: _____

Academic knowledge (about planets, dinosaurs, math, etc.): _____

_____

Artistic skills (drawing, painting, sculpting, etc.): _____

_____

Handy skills (ability to fix flat tires, faucets, etc.): _____

_____

Outdoor skills (putting up a tent, building a fire, etc.): _____

_____

Performance skills (singing, juggling, acting, etc.): _____

_____

Personal experiences (escaping a burning building, etc.): _____

_____

Sports skills (hitting a baseball, jumping rope, etc.): _____

_____

Travel (interesting or unusual places visited or lived in): _____

_____

Other knowledge (write on the back or on another sheet):

TALKING ZOO

A good way to understand anything is to experience it from the inside. This is especially true when studying animals.

DIRECTIONS:

1. Have students create animal "houses" for a classroom zoo. Try using refrigerator boxes, with black crepe paper for the bars. Or simply hang crepe paper from a clothesline hung across the room.

2. Divide the class into small groups, each of which chooses an animal on which to report.

3. Group members should gather as much information as they can about their animal from books and magazines. They might also call or write the nearest zoo, or interview a veterinarian.

4. Students next make paper-plate masks (see model masks on pages 97-99) or full-scale costumes. One member of each group will act as the zoo keeper while others become the animals.

5. Other students from the class should question the animals about their diets, habitats, and other characteristics. Later, invite younger students to visit the zoo and "talk to the animals."

EXTENSION:

Have each group write a play about its animal. This might simply take the form of an interview, or it could involve a real plot, for example, "The Day a Camel Came to Class."

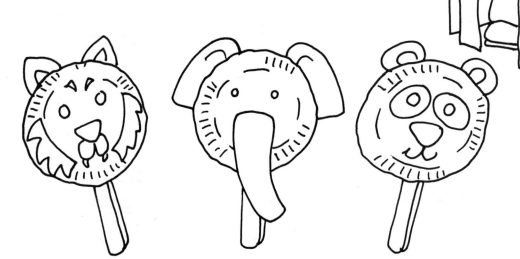

Animal Mask: Elephant

Animal Mask: Panda

Animal Mask: Tiger

TELEVISION DOCUMENTARY

Programs such as "60 Minutes" and "20/20" demonstrate how to use TV for studying current events. Thanks to lightweight camcorders, even young children can produce video accounts of phenomena in and around the school.

DIRECTIONS:

1. Make sure students understand what a TV documentary is: a program that shows and explains a real event, such as a parade, or a process, such as the building of a house. Usually, an unseen narrator describes what's shown on the screen. One way to introduce the concept of a documentary is to play a videotape of a professionally produced documentary.

2. Go over the steps in producing a TV show (page 123).

3. Divide the class into documentary teams (production units) or do a whole-class documentary.

4. Stick with doable topics, for example, documenting a "Day in the Life of a Baby Robin" makes sense . . . if a robin's nest happens to be outside your window.

5. Have students list what they want to shoot before they begin. Random taping usually spells disaster. During the recording, it's OK to add unexpected material. But for best results, keep programs short—five minutes or less.

6. Be ready to help the teams trouble-shoot their productions. Remind students that problems and mistakes are an important part of the learning process.

7. Have each team evaluate its program, listing strengths and weaknesses.

8. Play the finished programs in class.

EXTENSION:

If your town has a cable system with a public access channel, arrange for your students' programs to be broadcast at a time when parents can see their work.

TESTING! TESTING!

Often the person who makes up a test learns more than the person who takes it. (That may be why teachers are so smart.)

DIRECTIONS:

1. Each student writes a short report.
2. Students swap papers.
3. Partners write comprehension questions based on each other's papers. The tests can be true/false, fill in the blank, multiple choice, or a combination.
4. Test writers also prepare an answer key.
5. Attach each quiz to its report. Then use the packages for reading comprehension materials.

EXTENSION:

Have students try out the quizzes on their parents.

THEMATIC MUSEUM

Creating specialized museums is a powerful strategy for sharing knowledge about places, such as rain forests, or eras, such as the rise of the railroads. This activity calls upon a variety of skills, including writing, drawing, and model making.

DIRECTIONS:

1. Have the entire class choose a theme for a museum, for example, forest animals. (See page 103 for more topics.)
2. Divide the class into groups, each of which will create a display or diorama related to the theme. For example, a forest museum might feature an owl exhibit, a spider exhibit, and a bear exhibit.
3. Students research their topics, making drawings and taking notes for the text that will accompany the physical display.
4. Each group uses a variety of media—stuffed animal toys, painted backdrops, natural objects (leaves, twigs)—to create a display.
5. Students draft text that explains their display. After revising and editing the rough draft, the final words are written on large pieces of poster board. (If you have a computer/printer setup, use it to generate eye-catching graphics.)
6. After the individual display areas are assembled, the whole class collaborates on an introductory display that tells visitors what to expect and how to move through the entire exhibit.
7. Have the whole class produce promotional posters and flyers inviting other groups to visit their museum.

EXTENSION:

Produce a TV show that takes viewers through the museum.

Museum Topics

African crafts

automobile history

classroom of the nineteenth century

clocks

colonial life

cooking artifacts

desert life

dinosaurs

endangered species

farm animals

household appliances

Indian village

ocean floor

pyramids

rain forests

spacecraft

volcanoes

weather

whales

writing implements

This is for our farm-animal museum.

TIME-LINE LESSONS

Historians try to make the past real. One way to do that is to visually represent historical events in a time-line: a series of chronologically-ordered pictures.

DIRECTIONS:

1. Divide the class into groups of about four students. Each group chooses a subject that spans a number of months or years, for example, Martin Luther King, Jr.'s life.
2. Each student in the group learns about one "point in time" contained in the subject. The student should also create a picture representing that moment.
3. During the presentation, line the students up and have them present their findings in chronological order.

EXTENSION:

Have students adapt their time-line lessons into traditional time-lines that can be hung up in the room, in the library, or along a hallway.

TRIALS AND TRUTHS

Being able to look at all sides of a controversial issue is the mark of an educated person. The following "legal" project gives students practice in weighing pros and cons.

Note: The trial format presented below is greatly simplified. For a more authentic view, share with your class the book *Beyond a Reasonable Doubt* by Melvyn Zerman (Crowell, 1981). Another option is to take a field trip to a court in session. Or invite a lawyer or judge to visit your class and explain the process.

DIRECTIONS:

1. Introduce the activity by having students read the sample trial script starting on page 106. Discuss the roles played by the judge, the prosecutor, the defense attorney, the witnesses, and the bailiff.
2. Divide the class into groups. Each group chooses a subject that has controversial aspects. Examples: cutting down forests, building nuclear power plants, and spending money on interplanetary travel. Consider subjects that seem bad, scary, or disgusting, but which have hidden benefits or at least intriguing aspects. Examples: bats, earthquakes, forest fires, maggots, mosquitoes, scabs, sharks, snakes, and spiders.
3. Members of the group research the topic and write a script in which the subject is on trial. As a pre-writing activity, brainstorm lists of questions that might be asked of each witness.
4. After writing and rehearsing the script, students present the trial to the whole class.
5. Classmates can serve as jurors to render the verdict.

EXTENSION:

Tape-record the trial so that you can share it with parents and with students in other schools.

Trial of a Mosquito

Judge: Prosecutor, would you please introduce your case.

Prosecutor: Ladies and gentlemen of the jury, I will prove to you that Mosquito is a horrible, worthless creature that should not be allowed to be around us.

Judge: Defense Lawyer, will you introduce your case.

Defense Lawyer: Thank you, Your Honor. Ladies and gentlemen of the jury, I will show you that Mosquito is an important part of our world and deserves our admiration, not our hate.

Judge: Prosecutor, you may call your first witness.

Prosecutor: I call Mosquito.

Bailiff: Will Mosquito please take the stand.

Mosquito: Here I come.

Bailiff: Do you promise to tell the whole truth and nothing but the truth?

Mosquito: Yes, I do.

Prosecutor: Do you buzz at night and keep people awake?

Mosquito: Well, my wings do make a sound that bothers some people. But I do not mean to disturb them. I just don't know how to fly without making a noise. It's the same with the jetliners that people use.

Trial of a Mosquito

Judge: Mosquito, just answer the question you were asked.

Mosquito: Sorry, Your Honor.

Prosecutor: Do you bite people?

Mosquito: Not exactly.

Prosecutor: Well, what do you do?

Mosquito: I puncture the skin with my proboscis.

Prosecutor: Your what?

Mosquito: My proboscis. It's a tube that is a kind of nose.

Prosecutor: What do you do after you puncture the skin?

Mosquito: I suck up a few drops of blood through my proboscis.

Prosecutor: That sounds horrible.

Mosquito: Maybe to you. But it's how I live. Did you ever look at what happens in your mouth when you're chewing food? Now *that's* disgusting.

Judge: Once again, we're not interested in your opinions, Mosquito.

Prosecutor: When you puncture someone's skin, it hurts.

Trial of a Mosquito

Mosquito: Not right away. I squirt out a chemical that kills the pain for a few seconds.

Prosecutor: But after you leave, the place begins to itch.

Mosquito: I can't help that.

Prosecutor: You also spread disease, like malaria.

Mosquito: I don't mean to. Malaria is caused by a tiny, one-celled animal found in the blood. When I go from one person to another, a bit of the diseased blood may get into the second person's blood.

Prosecutor: And if that blood is infected, what happens?

Mosquito: The person might get the disease.

Prosecutor: So you cause the disease.

Mosquito: I don't mean to.

Prosecutor: No further questions, Your Honor.

Judge: Your witness, Defense Lawyer.

Defense Lawyer: If you didn't suck blood from people, what would happen?

Mosquito: I would starve to death.

Defense Lawyer: So you suck blood simply to stay alive. It's a matter of life and death.

Trial of a Mosquito

Mosquito: Yes.

Defense Lawyer: I have no more questions.

Bailiff: Mosquito, you may leave the stand.

Judge: Do you have any more witnesses, Prosecutor?

Prosecutor: No. I rest my case.

Judge: Defense Lawyer, you may call your witness.

Defense Lawyer: I have just one, River Scientist.

Bailiff: Will River Scientist please step forward.

River Scientist: Here I am.

Bailiff: Do you promise to tell the whole truth and nothing but the truth?

River Scientist: Yes.

Defense Lawyer: What is a food chain?

River Scientist: It's when one animal eats another and that animal is eaten by another one.

Defense Lawyer: Can you give me an example?

River Scientist: Sure. People eat big fish. Big fish eat little fish. That's a food chain.

Defense Lawyer: What do little fish eat?

Trial of a Mosquito

River Scientist: Some of them eat mosquito larvae. Larvae are what we call young mosquitoes.

Defense Lawyer: What would happen if there were no mosquitoes?

River Scientist: Then many kinds of fish would not survive.

Defense Lawyer: In other words, mosquitoes are important for the well-being of some fish?

River Scientist: That's true.

Defense Lawyer: And because people eat some of these fish, people depend on mosquitoes.

River Scientist: You could say that.

Defense Lawyer: I have no further questions.

Judge: Prosecutor, you may ask questions.

Prosecutor: River Scientist, do you like it when a mosquito drills into your skin and sucks up your blood?

River Scientist: No.

Prosecutor: You dislike this even though you know some fish depend on mosquitoes.

River Scientist: That's right.

Prosecutor: When you see a mosquito sucking your blood, what do you do?

Trial of a Mosquito

River Scientist: I squash it if I can.

Prosecutor: No further questions.

Bailiff: River Scientist, you may step down.

Judge: Prosecutor, you may sum up your case.

Prosecutor: Ladies and gentlemen of the jury, mosquitoes cause pain and spread disease. You must bring in a verdict that says they are guilty.

Judge: Defense Lawyer, it's your turn.

Defense Lawyer: Mosquitoes do cause some pain, and sometimes they cause disease, but they don't mean to do harm. Also, they enable many creatures to live. You must find Mosquito innocent.

Judge: Ladies and gentlemen of the jury, you have heard both sides. Now you must decide: Should Mosquito be sent away or be allowed to live among us?

You must decide.

WORKSHOP REPORTS

According to an old saying, "To teach is to learn twice." In the following activity, students use the hands-on approach to teach (and learn) valuable skills.

DIRECTIONS:

1. Divide the class into groups of four or five students.

2. Each group chooses a skill or process that relates to a curriculum area. For example, if the class has been studying the colonial period, processes might include weaving, candle making, canning fruits, making butter, and creating simple crafts. (See page 113 for more workshop topics.)

3. Each group researches its chosen process and practices the activity. Then students create a lesson plan for teaching the rest of the class how to do the process. The plan might list:

- objective—what they want the audience to be able to do
- materials needed
- visual aids—diagrams and samples of finished product, if any
- script to follow during the presentation

4. Each group should practice its presentation before leading the whole class through the lesson. During the workshop, group members should circulate and offer help to individuals or groups trying to master the skill.

5. Have each student complete a workshop evaluation form (page 114). Students should then share their evaluations with their partners.

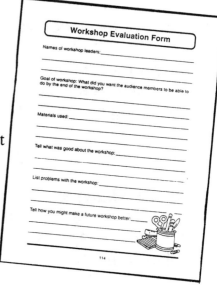

EXTENSION:

Each group adapts its lesson as a how-to-do-it TV show. Send videotapes home for the edification of family members.

Workshop Topics

Art

learning to draw a particular kind of object

making origami figures

making potato-block prints

shading

Language arts

correcting run-on sentences

looking for spelling patterns—such as "ei" after "c"

trying to solve a code or rebus

using a thesaurus or other reference book

writing a new kind of poem

Math

creating tangram figures

making graphs

measuring objects using both the English and the metric systems

Science

creating a color wheel

creating a replica of a nest

experimenting with ice cubes

learning to use a simple microscope

making a compass

making an electric magnet

testing the sensitivity of nerves

wiring up a simple battery-powered electric circuit

Social studies

building a model (wigwam, airplane, boat)

recreating an artifact from a particular period (braided rug, sundial, or knot used on a sailing ship)

writing and taking a poll

Workshop Evaluation Form

Names of workshop leaders:_____

_____

_____

Goal of workshop: What did you want the audience members to be able to do by the end of the workshop?

_____

_____

Materials used:_____

_____

_____

Tell what was good about the workshop:_____

_____

_____

List problems with the workshop:_____

_____

_____

Tell how you might make a future workshop better:_____

_____

_____

Resources

RESEARCH TIPS

Authentic research is creative. It has nothing to do with mindlessly copying from reference books. Rather, it's driven by curiosity and questioning. The following tips may help students grasp the basics of this vital skill.

1. Have students regularly write questions in their journals. Examples are: What makes a rainbow? Can cats learn to read? Why do some people run faster than others? Is it fun being a twin? Do blind people see anything when they dream? Inviting students to share questions may stimulate more questions. (It's helpful if the teacher shares, too.)

2. Sometimes have students choose research topics from their journals.

3. Before starting their research, students should write down what they already know about the topic, plus questions they want to answer.

4. Encourage students to try all three research methods:
   - using books, tapes, and other information packages
   - observing firsthand
   - interviewing experts

5. Teach about the library by pairing older and younger students. Each "senior" researcher will take a "junior" on a library tour. This will reinforce the older student's knowledge while introducing the younger student to the library's resources. Hint: For best results, the older student should script and rehearse the tour ahead of time.

The 500s are books about science.

6. Teach students the two secrets of note taking:
   - Don't write down what you already know (for example, that cows have four legs). Think about what will be news to the audience.
   - Put ideas into your own words. (For practice on paraphrasing, see page 69.)

7. After students draft their reports, provide time for testing their material with trial readers. (See page 117 for feedback strategies.)

Getting Feedback

After you write a rough draft for a report, share it with a trial reader. The following steps may help you learn ways to improve your work.

Step 1. Share your writing with your trial reader. You can do this by letting the person read your work. Or you can read it aloud while the person listens.

Step 2. Ask your reader questions, and take notes on the answers. Some questions you might ask are:

- Does the title make sense? Can you think of something better?
- Do you understand the main idea of the report? What do you think it is?
- Did the beginning interest you?
- Did any parts confuse you?
- What facts were new to you?
- What facts did you already know?
- Did the illustrations help you understand the report?
- Can you think of anything that should be added?
- Did the ending seem like a real ending to you?
- Do you have any other suggestions for making the report better?

Step 3. Use what you learned from your partner to review your report and make changes that you agree with. (You don't have to make a change just because your partner suggested it.)

LEARNING THE LIBRARY

Many of the activities in this book require library research. Unfortunately, some children are intimidated by the library. Yet, it's relatively easy to help them feel more comfortable there. Here are several strategies to instill student confidence.

1. Take a field trip to the library.
This works best if you plan a real itinerary. Guide the students through each section. Give particular attention to visiting each of the 10 Dewey Decimal sections.

2. Demonstrate how books are found.
Brainstorm a few topics with your students: insects, bicycle repair, recycling, magic tricks. Then, have an aide or older student take small groups to the library and show how books on these topics can be found using the index system.

3. Arrange for information scavenger hunts.
A scavenger hunt can make learning library basics into a game. The "Dewey Decimal Scavenger Hunt" sheet (page 119) asks students to locate an example of a book in each category of the system. The "Reference Book Scavenger Hunt" sheet (page 120) aims to help students become familiar with several key research resources. You might ask older students to list one fact from each book on the back of the scavenger sheet or on another piece of paper. With younger students, you might organize the hunt as a group project, perhaps with an older student serving as guide. The "Parts of a Book Scavenger Hunt" sheet (page 121) helps students, especially beginning researchers, discover the key elements of most nonfiction books.

4. Map the library.
Creating maps is a good way to understand the layout of the library. This can be an excellent small-group project.

118

Dewey Decimal Scavenger Hunt

Most libraries put nonfiction books into 10 groups. In the library, find one book for each group. Write its title and number in the space.

000-099 General works

Title and number_____

100-199 Ideas

Title and number_____

200-299 Religion

Title and number_____

300-399 Social sciences

Title and number_____

400-499 Languages

Title and number_____

500-599 Pure sciences

Title and number_____

600-699 Useful sciences

Title and number_____

700-799 Arts

Title and number_____

800-899 Literature

Title and number_____

900-999 History and geography

Title and number_____

Reference Book Scavenger Hunt

Most libraries have books that help people find facts fast. These books are called reference books. In your library, find an example of the following kinds of reference books. Write the exact title of the book. Then, briefly tell what subject or subjects the book is about.

Almanac

Title: _____

Subject: _____

_____

Atlas

Title: _____

Subject: _____

_____

Dictionary

Title: _____

Subject: _____

_____

General encyclopedia (set of books)

Title: _____

Subject: _____

_____

Parts of a Book Scavenger Hunt

This page can help you get to know the parts of a book. To do the activity, you need a nonfiction book.

1. The title page is the first or second page in a book. It tells the name of the book. It also tells who wrote it (author) and the company that made (published) it.

Title of your book: _____

Author or authors of your book: _____

Publisher of your book:_____

2. The copyright page comes next. It tells the year the book was published.

The copyright year of your book is:_____

3. The contents page lists the chapters in a book. How many chapters does your book have? _____

What is the first chapter called?_____

4. Check each kind of picture found in your book:
( ) color drawings   ( ) black and white drawings
( ) color photographs ( ) black and white photographs
( ) maps   ( ) diagrams

5. A glossary defines special words used in the book. Does your book have a glossary? ( ) yes   ( ) no

If it does, list one word in the glossary:_____

6. An index tells the pages where you can find different topics. Does your book have an index? ( ) yes   ( ) no

If it has an index, list one word in the index: _____

AUDIO TIPS

Several of the projects described in this book use tape recorders. Many others can be extended through the use of audiotape. The following tips are designed to enable students to produce quality audio programs.

1. Practice using the microphone. Before recording real programs, students should make experimental tapes. They can read newspaper articles, excerpts from textbooks, etc. Demonstrate how to talk directly into the microphone from close up—about six inches (12 centimeters).

2. Keep the programs short! One of the worst mistakes any media person can make is to ramble. Listeners quickly lose interest. Few elementary-age students can create a quality audio presentation that lasts more than two or three minutes.

3. Work from scripts. Improvisation can be extremely difficult for students to pull off. Usually, it leads to a disorganized presentation. If students invest time and effort in writing scripts, they will be well on their way to creating a quality product. Another bonus: using the script approach gives practice in writing clear prose.

4. Rehearse. Running through a script two or three times is the most important strategy for achieving excellence.

5. Find a quiet place to make recordings. Inexpensive tape recorders, especially those with built-in microphones, tend to pick up background noise. To avoid a distracting din, have students tape their programs in a quiet room, preferably one with a carpet. If this is not possible, you might arrange for them to make tapes in the classroom while the rest of the students are at recess. Hint: Warn students not to rustle their scripts when recording. Old-time radio pros developed the trick of keeping their scripts unbound, and dropping each page as they finished reading it.

6. Listen to finished programs and talk about their strengths and weaknesses. Focus on questions like "How could this have been improved?" or "What can be done next time to create a better program?"

7. Carefully mark the cassettes containing finished programs. Nothing is more frustrating than trying to find a show in a box of unmarked tapes.

VIDEO TIPS

As the cost of lightweight camcorders (video cameras) continues to drop, chances for student-made television will increase.

Video in school has two main benefits: it enables students to see themselves as reporters; and it lets students capture and share what they see. Neither benefit requires fancy equipment. More than hi-tech, students need to learn a few common-sense fundamentals. Try the following.

1. Experiment with equipment before making a real show. Divide the class into groups and show them the basics. Allow each student to run the camera for about 15 seconds and evaluate the results. The key camera skill is steadiness. Whenever possible, the camera should sit on a tripod. Panning (side to side motion) and zooming (in and out motion) make viewers dizzy and should be avoided. Allow the on-camera talent to provide the action.

2. Keep programs short! Usually, the longer the program, the lower the quality. Students will do better if their efforts are limited to five minutes or less.

3. Work from scripts. The great majority of professionals depend on highly detailed scripts. A useful script will describe visuals (what appears on screen) and sounds (words, music, noises). Hint: using an off-screen narrator is a simple strategy for making programs seem more professional.

4. Encourage students to create backdrops. These can be as simple as a drawing of trees for a nature program, or as complex as a set for an interview show. Even simple sets, which don't look like much "live," tend to be impressive when viewed on the TV screen.

5. Rehearse. If highly experienced news pros read over their scripts before going on the air, so should your students. Rehearsals should also involve the camera operator and other crew members.

6. Evaluate programs. Celebrate what makes them good, and try to learn how future shows might be improved.

7. Label the cassettes. This way you'll have them handy when you need them.

ILLUSTRATING REPORTS

Students don't need the skills of a da Vinci to visually enrich a report. The key is knowing about the forms that illustrations can take. While gaining mastery requires years of practice, even beginners can create illustrations that convey real information. Here are several starting points.

1. Have students collect examples of functional art used in newspapers, magazines, textbooks, nonfiction books, and packaging. Sort the illustrations into categories:

- diagrams
- drawings
- maps
- photographs

Point out the use of words in captions and labels. Sum up what you learn in a bulletin board about illustration.

2. Give students drawing practice by having them make simple drawings of everyday objects. Begin with flat items, such as leaves, paper clips, keys, zippers, calculators, or coins. Then try head-on views of more complicated objects, such as pencil sharpeners, telephones, and models of cars and planes. Have students label the parts.

3. Practice making maps of limited areas, such as the classroom or the playground. If you have access to a doll house with a removable roof, use it as a "prompt" for drawing floor plans.

4. One way to learn to draw more complicated objects is to copy—but not trace—drawings found in books. Tracing is a process used by professional artists, but it doesn't do much for developing the eye.

5. Encourage students to include illustrations in their actual reports.

6. Occasionally have students create illustrations for each other. This division of labor can help students see the value of illustrations.

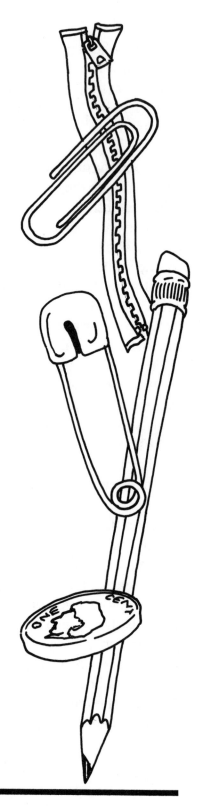

READING LIST

Children's libraries and bookstores feature many books on research and reporting. While the books described here are good, if you can't find these titles, you and your students will probably be able to locate comparable ones. The majority of the books are written at the intermediate level. Most could be successfully read aloud to younger children. Several of the most interesting titles are picture books, written in simple prose.

BULLETIN BOARDS

Pin It, Tack It, Hang It: The Big Book of Kids' Bulletin Boards by Phyllis Fiarotta and Noel Fiarotta (Workman, 1975). Gives step-by-step directions for constructing bulletin boards using a variety of materials.

DRAWING

Aldo's Doghouse: Drawings in Perspective by Lee Savage (Coward, McCann, 1978). Uses a cartoon magician to explain the principles of three-dimensional drawing.

Drawing Book: Make a World by Ed Emberley (Little, Brown, 1972). Gives tips for drawing animals.

The Way to Draw and Color Dinosaurs by Don Bolognese and Elaine Raphael (Random House, 1991). Shows would-be artists how to draw dinosaurs walking, swimming, and flying. The book includes professional secrets, such as using tracing paper to merge different sketches into a big scene.

LETTER WRITING

Girls and Boys Write-a-Letter Book by Stan Tusan (Grossett, 1971). Presents tips for writing business letters, invitations, thank-you notes, and other letter forms.

Messages in the Mailbox: How to Write a Letter by Loreen Leedy (Holiday House, 1991). Discusses the parts of a letter, and gives ideas for finding people to write to.

LIBRARIES

Check It Out! The Book About Libraries by Gail Gibbons (Harcourt, 1985). Uses the picture-book format to present the benefits of libraries, and explains how to find resources via printed and computer catalogs. The book stresses the value of bringing one's questions to the library.

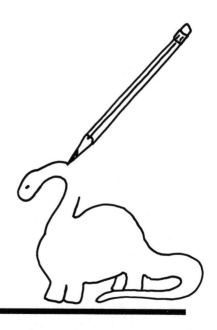

READING LIST

MAPS AND GLOBES

Looking at Maps by Erich Fuchs (Abelard-Schuman, 1976). Explains orientation, scale, symbols, and other map topics. Also included is a gallery of product maps, physical maps, weather maps, historical maps, and blueprints.

Map Making by Karin Mango (Messner, 1984). Explores astronomical maps, weather maps, and even fantasy maps. Skills include observing, charting, compass reading, and sketching. It also shows how to map a neighborhood.

Maps and Globes by Jack Knowlton (Harper, 1985). Gives a brief history of map making, and tells how to read all sorts of maps and globes.

MUSEUMS

African Crafts by Judith Corwin (Watts, 1990). Shows how to make traditional African designs, beads, board games, cloth, dolls, masks, and other artifacts.

Are Those Animals Real?: How Museums Prepare Wildlife Exhibits by Judy Cutchins and Ginny Johnson (Morrow, 1984). Reveals museum methods for creating underwater dioramas, dinosaur displays, and other exhibits. Readers learn how clay, plastic, rubber, and other materials are used to make lifelike foxes, swans, and other animals.

Dinosaurs Down Under by Caroline Arnold (Clarion, 1990). Describes how a museum exhibit, on loan from Australia, is shipped, assembled, and displayed in a U.S. museum.

Let's Be Early Settlers with Daniel Boone by Peggy Parish (Harper, 1967). Gives steps for creating quilts, brooms, quill pens, spinning wheels, fireplaces, and other items for use in dioramas or living museums.

Model Satellites and Spacecraft by Frank Ross, Jr. (Lothrop, 1968). Tells the stories of these engineering marvels and shows how to make them.

READING LIST

PUPPETS

Jim Henson: From Puppets to Muppets by Geraldine Woods (Dillon Press, 1987). Tells the story of the man and the team behind the Muppets, and how Henson's creations came to star in movies, on TV, and on the stage.

Making Easy Puppets by Shari Lewis (Dutton, 1967). Gives simple directions for creating and using 30 puppets, including an egg-head Santa and a folded-paper fish.

Plenty of Puppets to Make by Robyn and Lauren Supraner (Troll, 1981). Features puppets made from index cards, cereal boxes, egg cartons, and paper plates. Many of the projects, such as elephant and other animal puppets, would work well in presenting science dramas.

Puppet Fun: Production, Performance and Plays by Nellie McCaslin (McKay, 1977). Shows how to make puppets from spoons, hammers, socks, pencils, hands, even lollipops. Formats include rod, shadow, sock, and glove puppets, plus giant puppets (kids wearing puppet-like costumes).

SCIENCE FAIRS

How to Do a Science Fair Project by Salvatore Tocci (Watts, 1986). Gives step-by-step strategies for creating projects. Topics include choosing a subject, performing an experiment, and creating a polished presentation.

Setting Up a Science Project by Ann Stepp (Prentice-Hall, 1966). Guides students through the entire process of sharing scientific information.

TELEVISION

How to Make Your Own Video by Perry Schwartz (Lerner, 1991). Explains all aspects of video production, starting with the concept that "you must have something to say." Topics include choosing a camcorder, seeing the way a camera sees, storytelling, lighting and sound, and editing. Samples include scripts, plus a "daily production schedule" for shooting a sixth grade field trip.

Television by Alice Fields (Watts, 1980). Gives background on the medium, and describes the different jobs that must be done to put a show on the air.

Index